Commonsense Cataloging

COMMONSENSE CATALOGING

A Manual for the Organization of Books and Other Materials
in School and Small Public Libraries

ESTHER J. PIERCY

SECOND EDITION

Revised by MARIAN SANNER

THE H. W. WILSON COMPANY   NEW YORK   1974

Library of Congress Cataloging in Publication Data

Piercy, Esther J
    Commonsense cataloging.

    Bibliography: p.
    1. Cataloging. I. Sanner, Marian, ed. II. Title.
Z693.P54   1974   025.3   73-7573
ISBN 0-8242-0009-8

Preface to the Second Edition

This revision of Commonsense Cataloging could not be issued without a tribute to Esther J. Piercy—a librarian with vision who dared to be practical. Her book exemplified this dual talent; it reflected the new trends in cataloging and, at the same time, advocated simple methods of bibliographic control of library collections. This reviser enjoyed twelve years of stimulating association with Esther Piercy, late Chief of Processing, Enoch Pratt Free Library, and considers it a privilege to have been invited to do the first revision of Commonsense Cataloging.

The reviser has retained the arrangement of the first edition, proceeding "from the general to the specific, from principles to practices." The chapters on Subject Cataloging and Audio-visual and Other Nonbook Materials have been expanded. The rules presented in this revision are based on those contained in the *Anglo-American Cataloging Rules* and in *Non-book Materials: the Organization of Integrated Collections*; many of the rules have been rephrased for simplicity but retain the principles enunciated in the two codes. Two appendixes highly regarded by reviewers of the first edition—Directions for Typing and Checklist of Individual Library Practices—have been revised only to reflect changes in the text.

It is the reviser's hope that this second edition will be another commonsense manual "for the organization of books and other materials."

I wish to express my appreciation to Margaret Marquart, Head of the Catalog Department at the Enoch Pratt Free Library, with whom I talked over many aspects of the book, and to my secretary, Isabella Mecinski, who typed the manuscript. Thanks are due to many other colleagues who shared ideas with me.

Baltimore, Maryland
September 1973

MARIAN SANNER
Chief of Processing
Enoch Pratt Free Library

5

Preface

This book is designed to be practical, to serve as a manual or handbook for the beginning cataloger, trained or untrained. If used as suggested, with the information and decisions of the individual library recorded in the checklist provided in Appendix V, it should also serve as the manual of practice for that library. Even though the author may prefer or recommend certain practices (indicated by starred items in the checklist), inevitably there will be local situations which make other practices preferable or necessary. For the sake of consistency within an institution and to speed succeeding catalogers' learning the history and procedures, recorded decisions are necessary.

In the subtitle, "the organization of books and other materials" is admittedly a lengthy phrase; nevertheless there is no shorter way to say what is meant. Libraries are no longer solely collections of books; books must be supported by other materials, including pamphlets, maps, records, periodicals, pictures, films, and other forms of communication. And, while cataloging and classification are the basic means of organizing materials, they are not the only methods of dealing with books, let alone the other materials. A library's collections should be as easily and fully used as possible, but the arrangements for this use should be made in the most expeditious way possible, that is, the most economical in time.

The terms "Processing," "Technical Services," and "Technical Processes" do not appear in the title since many of the services generally included in these terms are not considered here. Excluded, for instance, are the selection and acquisition of materials; their shelving, care, and housing; and their control (circulation, registration, etc.). The physical preparations (pasting, stamping, lettering, jacketing, etc.) *are* included because this work is part of cataloging in many libraries and because many questions of cataloging and preparations are solved together.

The school libraries for which this manual is intended include those in elementary, junior high, and senior high schools, general and special. Defining "the small public library" is more difficult, but in general the concern is primarily with those libraries in communities of 10,000 or fewer people and those not expected to expand greatly in the foreseeable future. Actually, however, the cataloging is appropriate for public libraries much larger. Whether the organization or processing is done within the walls of the individual library or done for it in some processing center, the *kind* of cataloging will be the same. Church libraries were not included in the original planning of this manual, but it developed that, with few exceptions, the practices recommended would also be suitable for church and parish libraries; these exceptions are therefore noted in the text.

The word "commonsense" is used because the hope is to dispel some of the fears, mystery, superstitions, and mystique which sometimes surround the word "cataloging." After all, all the librarian has to do is decide, first, what purposes the collection is intended to serve, and then how best to organize the materials to perform the services.

In making such decisions he is conforming with recent movements and evaluations. The last few years have seen the publication of many sets of standards, the most pertinent being those for school libraries, public libraries, and the small public library. The American Library Association rules for form of entry, the ALA-LC rules for descriptive cataloging, and the ALA rules for filing are in the process of revision. The practices recommended herein observe the principles enunciated for these revisions, but are adapted to conform with the best practices developed for school and public libraries over the past twenty years.

COMMONSENSE CATALOGING differs from many similar works in this field not only in the features which make possible its adoption as a manual for each library, but also in its over-all arrangement. It is deliberately designed to go from the general to the specific, and from principles to practices, in the belief that before one can work effectively, one must have one's purposes clearly defined, that one must see the picture whole before undertaking the specific tasks. An attempt has been made to keep the text less tedious by removing routine matters and incorporating them in the Appendixes; thus it is hoped that the prospective cataloger will be persuaded to read the entire text before starting work—he will surely save time in the long run by doing so.

As usual with even so simple a work, many people have become involved at various stages and have made contributions. From the Wayne County Public Library have come some of the card samples used. And gratitude must be expressed to those who have read different drafts of the work and made careful suggestions; they have eliminated many mistakes and strengthened the whole. People who took the time to give this generous help include Virginia Drewry of the Georgia State Department of Education; Claribel Sommerville and the catalogers at the Public Library of Des Moines, Iowa; Eloise Rue and James Krikelas of the University of Wisconsin, Milwaukee; Mary V. Gaver and Paul S. Dunkin of the Graduate School of Library Service of Rutgers—The State University, New Jersey; Ruth French Strout of the Graduate Library School of the University of Chicago; and Audrey Smith of the Free Library of Philadelphia. Gertrude Samuels, Marian Sanner, and the other catalogers at the Enoch Pratt Free Library have, of course, talked out many points and answered endless questions.

Baltimore, Maryland
April 1965

ESTHER J. PIERCY

Table of Contents

Procedures and Preliminaries 1

Background Information

Anyone planning to make use of this book would be well advised to read it through, noting that there is more than one way to do most things in cataloging and in organizing a collection. After a careful reading of the whole, one is ready to start over, studying each chapter and the corresponding checklist in Appendix V. Whether the individual library is a new one just being organized or an older one with records and procedures established, it is advisable to think through the whole procedure, decide what is best, and make plans to act accordingly. No procedure is ever so perfect as not to profit from searching inspection, and no change can be made in the future so well as in the present since it is assumed that any library worth organizing is going to grow and keep on growing.

The procedures and decisions chosen for each particular library are those best for that library, and to decide what is best (that is, what is wanted and needed and economically sound), the catalog must be looked at in terms of its place in the library and the library's place in its institution or community. Therefore some preliminary information is needed, gathered through consultation with co-workers, authorities, the administration, and the governing body; through study of the community; and through concentrated thought. Such background information should include:

1. The present size of the community served (town, county, school, or church, as the case may be).
2. The community's potential size. Is it growing rapidly, steadily, or not at all?

3. The size and potential size of the library. What is its organizational pattern? Is it now, or is it likely to become, part of a larger system? What is its relationship to the system? What is likely to be its relationship? Does the system now have centralized processing? If not, is it being planned, or does it seem to be a logical future development?

4. The circulation system employed. Is any change contemplated? (Much of the work of preparing books and materials for use must be coordinated with the way they are charged out.) Are book cards used? Date-due slips?

5. The policy regarding lost books. Is the borrower charged for the loss? Is he charged actual library cost, the list price, or something more than list price to pay for processing? Or is a flat charge made? Is this policy the same for adults and children?

6. Any city, school, or church restrictions (established by law or policy) affecting the work. For instance, is an accession record required? Special accounting? Inventory accounting? Report or other forms prescribed? What statistics are required? Is there a manual or record of procedural decisions or recommendations?

7. The people served. Does the library serve primarily (or only) adults or children? If children are served, of what age?

8. Type of service. Is the library used primarily (or exclusively) either for reference or for circulating materials? Does it take an active part in educational activities, directly or indirectly?

9. The other library resources of the community.

10. The library's relationship to school supervisors, county or state library agencies, or other supervisory and advisory bodies.

11. Shelving policies. Are all books on open shelves or is part of the collection in closed stacks? If the latter, what proportion? What categories?

12. The book-buying policy. Are books bought on contract? Bids? Ordered once a year? Twice a year? Monthly? Weekly?

13. The policies on accepting gifts of books; of other materials.

14. Special collections or rooms. Are any special collections maintained? If so, are they separately housed or shelved? Separately indexed or cataloged?
15. Audio-visual and other nonbook materials. What types are acquired? How are they used? Do they circulate? To whom?
16. The library's discard and replacement policies. For example, does it keep only latest editions of informational books?
17. Duplication of material. Is the policy to have many copies of few titles or few (even single) copies of many titles? Are paperbacks used as duplicates?
18. A thorough examination of the catalog and shelf list, and a careful reading of existing policies and procedures.

After the prospective cataloger has collected and thought through such information and decisions, he is ready to read through this book, record his decisions in Appendix V, and thus convert the book into a manual for his own library. The process should prepare him for more intelligent work and should make for more uniform and consistent practice, both for himself and his successors. It is very easy to forget details and impossible to pass all of the information on to others if it is not written down. Furthermore, writing procedures down requires sharper thought and more definite decisions.

Planning the Work

Ideally, establishing cataloging procedures and decisions is best done at the beginning, that is, with a new library or a new collection. However, the cataloger (the term "cataloger" is used for anyone doing the work even though the cataloging is only a part of his work) nearly always must do his work in a library in which practices have been established, must decide what is best for the library, and then consider his strategy. He has several choices: (1) he can follow precedent, (2) he can "adapt" old practices to new (that is, compromise or combine), (3) he can do over what has been done, or (4) he can ignore the old (expecting it to be discarded ultimately) and start anew.

His decision as to the course to be followed is based on the questions listed at the beginning of this chapter, and also on the size of the collection, how appropriate and competent has been the former work, and what is feasible in time and money. Although it is foolish to continue bad practices, compounding the errors and building toward future recataloging, it is also unwise to assume immediately that all of the past is bad and begin something one cannot finish or something which will keep the catalog in a turmoil for a long period.

Sometimes shortcuts can be employed in adapting old to new. For instance, one can line out old subject headings on cards and write in new ones above, assuming that such unsightly cards will sooner or later be withdrawn. Sometimes a history card or a cross reference (see pages 158-161) will tie the old and new together. The important thing is to decide why things were done as they were, what will be gained by a change, and what is the best and simplest way to effect the change. If one is a newcomer to cataloging or new to the library, it is safest to wait a few months for self-education before making drastic changes.

It is also necessary to keep in mind the possibilities of the individual library's becoming part of a larger system or joining a processing center. No cataloging or preparations procedures should be adopted which will make future cooperation difficult. It is wise to adopt the practices of the nearest libraries of similar type and size, if these practices are well-defined and logical. Perhaps it is well to do no cataloging until the pattern is clear. In the interim the books could be arranged in large groupings, such as "Literature," "Sports," "Religion," and so forth, with no catalog. If noncataloging would be a serious impediment to use of the collection during the interim, the best procedure would be adherence to present practices until satisfactory policies can be developed.

The public library standards recommend that a library not undertake its own processing if it is not large enough to keep a full-time cataloger busy, and the school standards recommend that a system of three or more schools centralize the processing work. The centralized processing movement is growing so rapidly and being pushed so unanimously that it may be considered inevitable. So it cannot be stressed enough that centralization should always be considered in terms of "when," not "if."

Tools for the Work

After the preliminary study, the librarian is ready to acquire the necessary tools for cataloging. The minimum for even the smallest library includes:

A list of subject headings
A classification schedule

A cataloging manual

The handbook of directions for ordering prepared cards

A manual of filing rules (if those in Appendix II are considered oversimplified)

The cataloger should have access to a good unabridged dictionary, an up-to-date encyclopedia, appropriate foreign dictionaries, and such book selection aids as the appropriate publication in the Standard Catalog series, the appropriate ALA *Basic Book Collection, The Booklist, Book Review Digest,* and *Publishers Weekly.* Larger libraries buying more adult books will also need a manual for applying the classification numbers, fuller rules of cataloging, more advanced cataloging texts, trade bibliographies, etc. (See Appendix IV.)

This manual touches only briefly on the classifying of materials and the application of subject headings, because the standard guides are necessities for the cataloger, and each has a good introduction explaining its use. The introductions must be studied carefully before any attempt is made to use the schemes.

Physical Organization

The next preparatory steps are acquiring the necessary equipment and supplies and organizing the work.

A desk and posture chair are necessary. If this is a one-man library, a separate desk should be provided in addition to the one on which orders are prepared, reports drafted, letters written, magazines and bibliographies checked, and all other work done. Even if the second "desk" is a kitchen table, it should be there in a quiet corner where the work can be spread out, and, in case of interruption, returned to. A typewriter is needed with a card platen. If one typewriter must serve all purposes, an extra platen can be purchased. (See Chapter 11 for further discussion.)

The work space should be not only comparatively secluded, but near a sink with running water. A second work table for preparing materials is also desirable; this provides a space on which to place books which have been cataloged and leaves the catalog desk free of preparation supplies.

A catalog case is necessary (two if children and adults are served with separate catalogs), the size depending on the size of the library, and the material and style depending on the library decor. In estimating the size of the catalog, one may figure a thousand cards to a drawer and five cards for each title. It must be a standard library card catalog, made by a regular library supply house. The work area should have additional files for the shelf-list record, authority cards, order records, etc. A paste pot and shellac pot, a small pasting machine, a sponge, a book truck or two, and some handy shelves and cupboards should round out the minimum equipment requirements.

As for supplies, the most important are the catalog cards (see Chapter 11 for a discussion of size and kind). As an estimate of the number of cards needed, it takes about five per volume (*not* title) to be added in a year's time. (There will be some duplication of titles, but the round number of five allows for shelf-list cards and for spoilage.) Of course, if printed cards are to be purchased, the number of plain ones needed will be proportionately smaller. Transparent book jackets, if used, must be selected and ordered (see Chapter 13); book cards, pockets, and date-due slips must be purchased—all are described in catalogs from library supply houses. Pens, pencils, inks, brushes, paper labels, paste, shellac, steel and other erasers, alcohol, discs or "spots" necessary for marking special categories of books, rubber stamps, and mending and other supplies can be purchased as needed from the library supply houses or from a local stationery store.

Organization of the Work

If the staff has more than one member, one person should have the responsibility for the cataloging and one for the typing and other clerical work under the cataloger's supervision. Definite time should be scheduled for the work, based on the pattern of ordering. That is, if books are ordered once or twice a year, full time may be needed to work on them when they arrive; if the flow is thin and spread throughout the year, a few hours a week may serve. Even in a one-man library, the librarian should schedule definite time to do the work, preferably when the library is closed. If he tries to attend to the public's needs and catalog at the same time, both activities suffer.

He should assemble his material in one place and plan to have the work move in a methodical way through the steps. For instance, he should have the books to be cataloged arranged alphabetically by author on a truck, and checked all at one time against the necessary files. If cards are being purchased but have not yet arrived, the books can either be put on a "wait" shelf (kept in alphabetical order) until the cards arrive, or, better, they can be classed and the order cards used as temporary records, releasing the books for use. In schools they can sometimes be held; in public libraries they will have to be prepared and released for circulation at once.

If all cards are to be typed, a work slip is prepared, written or typed, indicating the information to be carried on the completed catalog card. Or, if the information on the order card is full enough to indicate the necessary information, it may serve as a work slip. When a sufficient number of books are assembled with the work slips or printed cards, they are ready for the cataloger. (The preliminary steps of ordering cards, preparing work slips, and assembling them with the matching books can be done by a clerical, student, or volunteer assistant.)

The cataloger checks the slips or cards against the books, indicating any corrections or changes, then assigns classification numbers from the classification scheme and assigns subjects from the headings book. Then, working with half a dozen at a time, he checks the work slips or cards against the catalog and the shelf list to make sure that the suggested entries, subjects, and classification numbers conform with previous practice. (See Chapters 3, 5, 7, and 8 for details of these processes.) When he has completed this work, the truckload of books is turned over to the typist for completion. The cataloger "revises" the work (that is, reads proof and indicates corrections) and removes the catalog and shelf-list cards from the books. The truckload of books is then ready for the page or student assistant who prepares the books: pasting in pockets, lettering the spines, stamping ownership, applying jackets, etc. This work is also checked by the cataloger or by an experienced clerk. These steps may be summarized:

Clerical or student assistant	*Cataloger*
1. Checks proposed order in catalog, indicating call number for duplicates	
2. Prepares order card	
	3. Reviews order
4. Completes and places order for books	
5. Orders printed cards for books	

Clerical or student assistant   *Cataloger*

6. When cards arrive, checks against books or records on hand, arranges cards for books not received alphabetically in card file
7. When books arrive, separates duplicates from new titles
8. Draws order cards; assembles shelf-list cards for duplicates, printed catalog cards for new titles
9. Stamps or letters accession numbers in books
10. Arranges books on truck with cards in books

11. Checks cards against books, indicating changes or indicating information for typing cards
12. Assigns classification number for each book
13. Assigns subject or subjects
14. Indicates other cards
15. Checks slips against shelf list and catalog
16. Pencils call number in book

(11-16 alternative if catalog cards have not yet arrived: Assigns classification number
Writes call number on order card and in book
Records statistical count
Sends book to Step 26)

17. Types headings and call numbers on printed cards or types full sets of cards
18. Enters accession information on shelf-list card

Clerical or student assistant	*Cataloger*
19. Types book card, pocket, and label	
	20. Revises typing of cards and label
	21. Removes catalog, shelf-list, and order cards from books
	22. Records statistical count
	23. Files shelf-list cards
	24. Discards order cards if no longer needed
	25. Puts catalog cards aside for filing
26. Pastes pocket and date-due slip in book	
27. Applies label to book jacket Applies jacket to book or Letters spine of book Shellacs book	
	28. Checks lettering and other preparations work
29. Shelves books	
30. Files cards in catalog above rod or with filing cards	
	31. Revises filing in catalog

The work space should be carefully planned for this progression. Every waste step is wasted time, and running back and forth checking one book at a time here and there is not only wasteful but tiring. *If* sized plastic jackets are used (see page 100), the measuring gauge should be attached to the wall near the jackets, which are grouped by size; after a group of books is measured, the jackets are pulled and laid in the books (the proper one in each), the books stacked on the work table, and all the jackets applied and pasted (or taped) in one sitting. Every step (no matter how trivial) should be planned with the same care. Doing half a dozen things at once on a cluttered work table or desk is inefficient and nerve-wracking.

Aids and shortcuts should be used freely, but big machines to do small jobs make no sense. If there is a choice in procedures, a few minutes of timing the different ways will usually provide the answer. Printed or processed forms and rubber stamps are true gold if used wisely. For instance, if reference books are cataloged but shelved behind the desk and the clerk must type or write again and again, "Ask at desk for this book," get a stamp. A small library, however, has neither time nor money nor facilities for testing more elaborate equipment or products; it is much wiser to read what has been done or to ask for advice. (See Chapter 13.*)

Organization Other than Cataloging

Although cataloging, classification, and the dictionary catalog comprise the type of organization of material primarily discussed in this manual, it must always be kept in mind that there are other ways of organizing or controlling library collections. The ALA standards for small libraries recommend book cataloging for all public libraries, but there is wide variation in the handling of materials other than books and of different collections. For some materials or collections it is best to classify and not catalog, to catalog and not classify, or to do neither. Although proposed use and most efficient service are the primary considerations, costs and time must also be considered. It is poor planning to spend a great deal of time on an elaborate control when a simpler method will serve equally well. To do so not only means waste but often means withholding material from use.

For example, such publications as college catalogs, trade catalogs, publishers' catalogs, and courses of study may well be shelved without any treatment except, perhaps, being stamped with the library's ownership. Only the latest edition of each is kept, older editions being discarded as they are superseded by new ones. Many reference books (encyclopedias, atlases, dictionaries, almanacs, directories, yearbooks, etc.) will be kept in one collection or else on stands and tables. Neither cataloging nor classification is necessary, although some marking (such as "R") is helpful for shelving purposes. If it seems desirable that the catalog indicate the presence of these reference works in the library, a form card may be prepared. (See Figure 1.)

---

* Also to be consulted is D. D. Dennis, *Simplifying Work in Small Public Libraries*. Philadelphia, Drexel Institute of Technology, 1965.

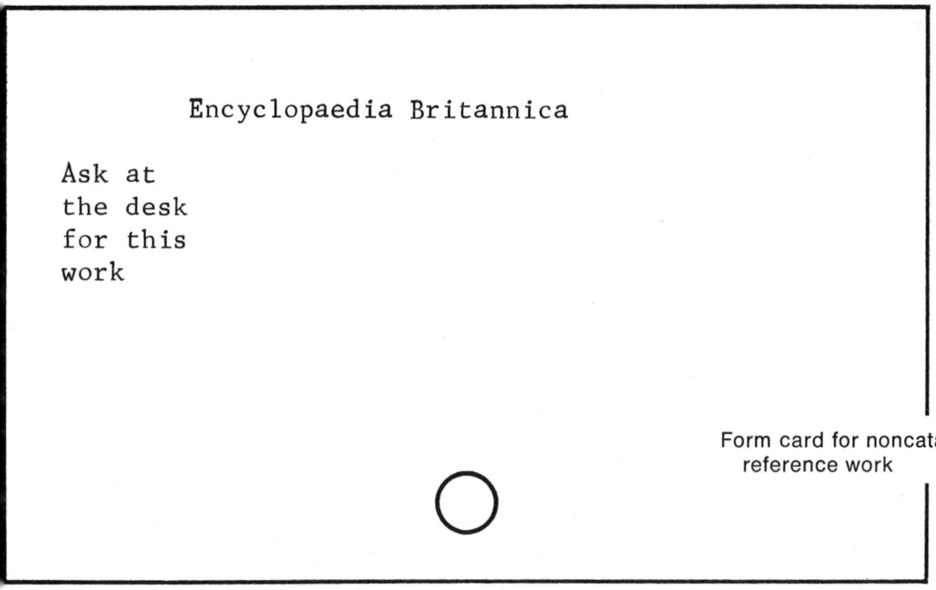

```
          Encyclopaedia Britannica

Ask at
the desk
for this
work

                                            Form card for noncataloged
                                                reference work
                        ◯
```

FIGURE 1

Audio-visual and other nonbook materials and their treatment are discussed in Chapter 14.

Library Publishers

Background information about some of the publishers specializing in library publications is helpful for the beginner:

1. The Library of Congress (commonly spoken of as LC) is the library organized for the use of the United States Congress in Washington. It is one of the largest libraries in the world, and the institutions it services have grown to include not only other Federal Government agencies, but also practically every library in the country; it is, in fact, the unofficial national library. Its librarians participate in all major library planning in the country; it publishes many aids and tools; and it offers various direct services, including the sale of printed catalog cards.

2. The American Library Association (ALA), as the largest association of American librarians, necessarily takes the lead in establishing library goals and standards, in urging governmental legislation for improving libraries and library services, in establishing and unifying library practices, and in conducting institutes and workshops. It also publishes reports, periodicals, studies, aids, and tools. Three of its divisions are particularly concerned with matters which are also of concern to users of this

manual: the American Association of School Librarians,* the Public Library Association, and the Resources and Technical Services Division. The last includes a Cataloging and Classification Section which speaks for ALA in this area of work.

3. The H. W. Wilson Company was founded in 1898 to serve libraries and the book world, first through its indexes (including, among many, the *Readers' Guide to Periodical Literature* and the *Cumulative Book Index*), then through other publications (including the Standard Catalog series and the *Wilson Library Bulletin*) and services, among them the sale of printed catalog cards. The company, its officers, and its employees work closely with libraries and library organizations for general library improvements and the improvement of its own services.

4. The R. R. Bowker Company (now a Xerox Company) is a publishing house which has served the book world, including libraries, since 1872. Its publications include *Publishers Weekly*, the *American Book Publishing Record*, the *American Library Directory*, *Library Journal*, *Books in Print*, and many other books and serials.

5. Others. The F. W. Faxon Company, Gale Research Company, the Scarecrow Press, the Shoe String Press, and the Special Libraries Association are among the other publishers who specialize in library aids. In addition, library schools are responsible for many magazines, serials, institutes, studies, and publications.

* Also an associated organization of the National Education Association.

The Card Catalog 2

The library catalog need not be a frightening thing, and its preparation should not be a goal in itself. It is a tool to serve the librarian and the library user; although it is the library's most important reference tool, it is still a tool. This means that it should contain only what is of predictable need and should eliminate all unnecessary embellishments, both as to what cards are included and what information is carried on the cards. No more time should be spent on it than necessary, but no information of value should be omitted.

There are various types of catalogs, but the type most widely used in the United States is the dictionary card catalog. Schools, public libraries, and other small libraries use the dictionary card catalog almost without exception, and it is the one with which we are concerned here. In this type of catalog all cards (or "entries") are in one file, alphabetically arranged by the first or filing name or word.

Book catalogs are coming into favor again, particularly in large libraries and library systems. However, for an individual small library they are expensive, will not give better access to the collection than a card catalog, and probably should not be considered.

The Catalog as Holdings Record

The catalog is not new; almost from the time that man, singly or in groups, started collecting books or their forerunners, he has felt the need to list the works to show him what he has. This remains the primary purpose of the catalog: to show what the library has. This the catalog does, and it must be prepared to do so, regardless of which of several pieces of information the user may have. He may know:

> the author of a work;
> the title of a work;
> the editor of a work;
> some other name or term associated with a work.

For each of these designations a card is made and filed in its alphabetical place under the key name or word. Thus the reader seeking a specific work quickly discovers whether or not it is in the library's collections.

The Catalog as Location Record

After the reader learns what the library has, the next information needed is, Where is the desired book located? Libraries have found the easiest way to answer this need is to assign a symbol to each book; the symbol will then serve as a device for shelving it in the desired order. If this symbol or device is carried on both the book and the catalog cards relating to it, the user may then be led directly from catalog card to book. It has also been found that by employing a subject classification scheme (see Chapter 8) books on the same subject can be brought together on the shelves, with books on related subjects close by. Thus the symbol, a subject classification number, serves two purposes: it locates a specific work and it brings it together with like materials. The user is led to the specific book desired, or he may browse through the books on the shelf which relate to the subject in which he is interested.

Reference Uses of the Catalog

Library practice has also discovered many reference uses for the card catalog, implicit both in deciding what cards are needed and in determining what information is to be included on the cards.

As to what cards are needed, the catalog may be expected to tell, in addition to the information discussed above:

1. What does the library have on a specific subject?
2. What titles by a given author does the library have? and
3. What books in a specific series does the library have?

Answers to the first question are provided by the use of subject headings (names, words, or phrases). Showing what the library has by a given author is done by providing cards under the name or names he has used in his works. The third question is answered by supplying a card under the name of a series for each title the library has in the series.

The information on the catalog card supplies a description of the individual work, such as who was responsible for its content, who published it and when, its size (number of pages or volumes), what it is about, and its relation to other works. (See Chapter 6.)

Cards in Sets

For each separate work cataloged a set of cards is prepared. Ordinarily, these will all be alike except for the top line, which carries the name, word, or phrase under which each card is filed. This use of a set of like cards is called the "unit" card system. One card is prepared which is called the "main entry"; this is usually the author card, and other cards are made which are exact copies of it except for the addition above the author's name of the various names, words, or phrases under which the additional cards will be filed. All cards other than the main entry card are "subject entry" and "added entry" cards. The number of cards required depends on the book itself (see Chapters 4 and 6) and may vary from one to twenty-five or more, the average being three to five.

The set of cards in Figure 2 is an example of the use of purchased printed cards. If printed cards are not used in the library or are not available for a specific title, the cards must be typed. In this case, shorter forms may be used for all of the cards except the main entry. (See Figure 3.)

Tracings on Cards

The cards will be scattered throughout the catalog, each under its own key filing or "entry" word. It is necessary therefore to know how many and what cards exist for each work in order to find them again to make corrections or to withdraw them when the title is no longer in the library. Therefore a means of finding or tracing these cards must be provided. This is done by listing all of the clues (filing names, words, or phrases) on the main entry card. These listings are called "tracings," appropriately enough. They appear on the face of the card if there is room, otherwise on the back.

There is an established practice for this listing. If on the face of the card, they are at the bottom and are arranged in paragraph

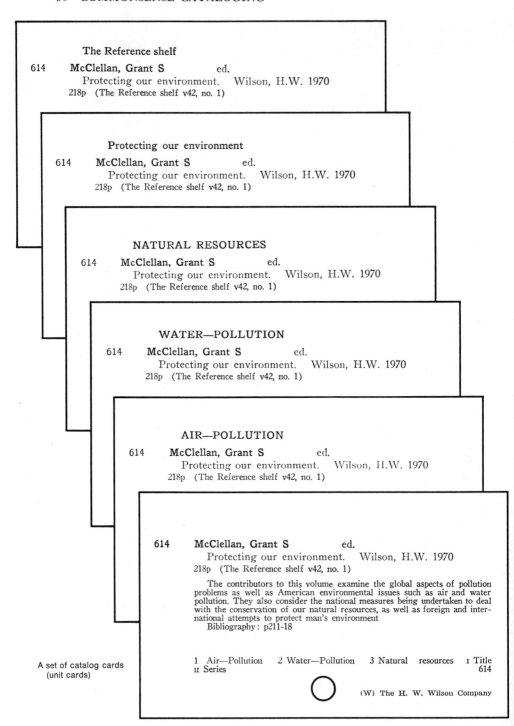

The Reference shelf

614   McClellan, Grant S   ed.
        Protecting our environment.   Wilson, H.W. 1970
      218p (The Reference shelf v42, no. 1)

Protecting our environment

614   McClellan, Grant S   ed.
        Protecting our environment.   Wilson, H.W. 1970
      218p (The Reference shelf v42, no. 1)

NATURAL RESOURCES

614   McClellan, Grant S   ed.
        Protecting our environment.   Wilson, H.W. 1970
      218p (The Reference shelf v42, no. 1)

WATER—POLLUTION

614   McClellan, Grant S   ed.
        Protecting our environment.   Wilson, H.W. 1970
      218p (The Reference shelf v42, no. 1)

AIR—POLLUTION

614   McClellan, Grant S   ed.
        Protecting our environment.   Wilson, H.W. 1970
      218p (The Reference shelf v42, no. 1)

614   McClellan, Grant S   ed.
        Protecting our environment.   Wilson, H.W. 1970
      218p (The Reference shelf v42, no. 1)

        The contributors to this volume examine the global aspects of pollution
      problems as well as American environmental issues such as air and water
      pollution. They also consider the national measures being undertaken to deal
      with the conservation of our natural resources, as well as foreign and inter-
      national attempts to protect man's environment
        Bibliography: p211-18

A set of catalog cards   1 Air—Pollution   2 Water—Pollution   3 Natural   resources   ɪ Title
(unit cards)   ɪɪ Series   614

                                                                        (W) The H. W. Wilson Company

FIGURE 2

or column form. If there is not room on the front, they are typed, one below the other, on the lower part of the back of the card (see Appendix I for typing directions). Tracings for subject entries come first and are designated by arabic numbers, with all other headings indicated by roman numbers. In typed tracings, the numbers may be omitted, but subjects are then typed in capital letters.

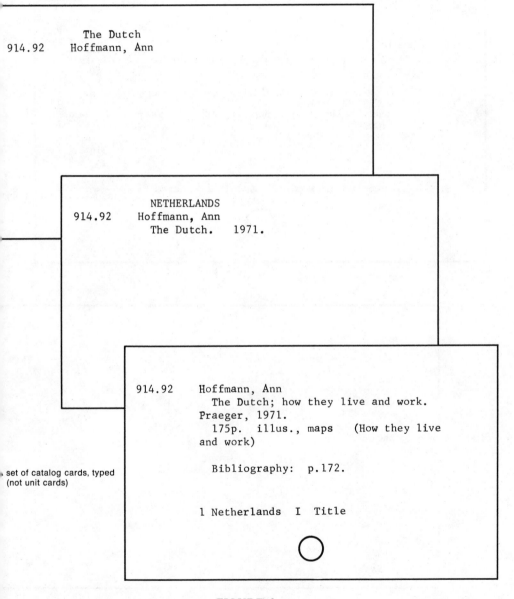

```
                    The Dutch
914.92      Hoffmann, Ann
```

```
                    NETHERLANDS
         914.92     Hoffmann, Ann
                        The Dutch.    1971.
```

```
         914.92     Hoffmann, Ann
                        The Dutch; how they live and work.
                    Praeger, 1971.
                        175p.  illus., maps    (How they live
                    and work)

                        Bibliography:  p.172.


                    1 Netherlands   I  Title
```

set of catalog cards, typed
(not unit cards)

FIGURE 3

That a card exists under the title of the work is shown by using the word "title" as a tracing. If there are two authors, the existence of a card for the second author is indicated by the abbreviation "jt. auth." The presence of a series entry is shown by the word "series" in the tracing.

380.5   Reische, Diana
        Problems of mass transportation.   Wilson, H.W. 1970
208p (The Reference shelf, v42, no.5)

    This compilation explores the crisis that now envelops mass transportation in the United States
    Contents: Is the situation hopeless; Villain of the piece: the beloved automobile; Commuting in Metropolis; Are passenger trains obsolete; Air travel: the problem is success; A look ahead; Bibliography

1   Transportation   2 Local transit   I Title   II Series   Printed card showing tracing

                (W) The H. W. Wilson Company

FIGURE 4

Tracings typed on back of
main entry card

1   Transportation
2   Local transit
I   Title
II   Series

FIGURE 5

Form of the Catalog Card

The decision as to how much and what information to supply on a card depends on its proposed use and hence on the size and service pattern of the individual library; but the form of the card itself, that is, the sequence of the information, follows uniform practice (see Chapter 6). This practice has been established through the years and has proved satisfactory. It takes into consideration readability, ease of preparation, assistance in preparing bibliographies, emphasis, and the requirements for adding necessary information as it later becomes available. (See Chapter 6 and Appendix I.)

If libraries follow the same form, it makes it easier to instruct people in the use of the catalog; it helps people in using different libraries; and it aids in the exchange of information between libraries. Also, it means that cards from various sources may be interfiled in the same catalog; future combining of library collections is possible with minimum effort; and later plans for cooperation between libraries are simplified.

Actual arrangement of information on the card (e.g., spacings and indentations) also has an established pattern, as set forth in Appendix I. But library catalogs today often include a mixture of printed, typed, machine-reproduced, and Xeroxed cards, and the form of the card is not sacrosanct. However, it is advisable to follow one form for typed cards so that the typist need not keep a variety of forms in mind.

The amount of bibliographic information (the book description) depends on the size of the collection (potential as well as present), a definition of its chief users (age, reading ability, interests), and its primary uses (school assignments, independent study or research, recreational reading, information reading, quick reference, and so forth).

3 The Main Entry

An entry is the name or word or phrase under which a card is filed or a bibliographic listing made. There are author entries, title entries, subject entries, illustrator entries, series entries, editor entries, and so forth.

The "main entry" is that name or term under which the work is primarily entered both on a catalog card and in a bibliography. The selection and the determination of the form in which it will be used (see Chapter 5 for form) are the most important parts of descriptive cataloging. It is by this main entry that a work will principally be known and the one by which it should most frequently be sought. If a book must be entered only once, as in a bibliography or union catalog, it will be by this main entry. All other names or phrases used as filing terms for that work then become "added entries" and "subject entries."

A few general principles form the basis of rules for selecting the main entry: (1) The entry is under the author if one can be determined. The term "author" is used to identify the person or corporate body responsible for the intellectual content of the work; thus the "author" may be an artist, a composer, or a photographer. (2) When there is no principal author, and an editor is responsible for the existence of a work, the main entry is under the editor. (3) In the case of a collection of works by various authors, the main entry is under the compiler. (4) Other works are entered directly under their titles.

The first step in cataloging a book is determining the main entry; the starting place for doing this is the title page, which carries the title and customarily includes the author statement. Other statements appearing on the cover, in the half title, or on the verso of the title page may be taken into account also. Information appearing only in the preface, introduction, or text is used in determining the main entry only when the title page and sources listed above lack sufficient information.

Personal Author as Main Entry

If a book is written by one person, his name is used as the main entry. Happily, most books are covered by this rule.

For example:
>*A title page reads:* Islands in the Stream. Ernest Heming-
>way.
>*The main entry would be:* Hemingway, Ernest

If there are two or three authors, the first name on the title page is usually selected as the main entry.

Examples:
>*Title page:* What to Do with Your Bad Car, by Ralph
>Nader, Lowell Dodge, Ralf Hotchkiss.
>*Main entry:* Nader, Ralph
>*Title page:* Dictionary of Word and Phrase Origins, by
>William and Mary Morris.
>*Main entry:* Morris, William

If a collection of the works of one person is edited by another, the main entry is under the author of the original works.

>*Title page:* The Poetry of Robert Frost. Edited by Ed-
>ward Connery Lathem.
>*Main entry:* Frost, Robert

However, a collection of the writings of various authors is entered under an editor or compiler, if one is named.

>*Title page:* A Treasury of Great American Speeches. Se-
>lected by Charles Hurd.
>*Main entry:* Hurd, Charles, comp.

A work which has been revised, enlarged, abridged, etc., by someone else is entered under the original author.

>*Title page:* Anatomy of the Human Body, by Henry
>Gray. 27th edition, edited by Charles Mayo
>Goss.
>*Main entry:* Gray, Henry

If, however, the new edition is obviously no longer the work of the original author, it is entered under the person responsible for the revision.

>*Title page:* Guide to Reference Books. 7th edition, by
>Constance M. Winchell. Based on the
>Guide to Reference Books, 6th edition, by
>Isadore Gilbert Mudge. (Completely re-
>vised, reorganized, and enlarged.)
>*Main entry:* Winchell, Constance M.

An adaptation, or a work rewritten in a different literary form, is entered under the adapter.

> *Title page:*   To Kill a Mockingbird, a full-length play
>   dramatized by Christopher Sergel, from
>   the book by Harper Lee.
> *Main entry:* Sergel, Christopher

A translation is entered under the author of the original work.

> *Title page:*   The Immoralist, by André Gide. Translated
>   from the French by Dorothy Bussy.
> *Main entry:* Gide, André

Corporate Body as Main Entry

Some works are issued by institutions, organizations, government bodies, or other collective groups. Examples of such bodies are Johns Hopkins University, Boy Scouts of America, United States Office of Education, and Conference of European Statisticians.

> *Title page:*   Boy Scout Handbook. 7th edition. Boy
>   Scouts of America.
> *Main entry:* Boy Scouts of America

A work which expresses the corporate thought or activity is entered under the corporate body even though it is prepared by an officer or employee.

> *Title page:*   A procedure for evaluating environmental
>   impact, by Luna B. Leopold, and others.
>   Geological survey circular 645.
> *Main entry:* U.S. Geological Survey

However, single reports written by individuals and resulting from scholarly research are entered under the personal author.

> *Title page:*   Subject Headings; a practical guide by David
>   Judson Haykin, Chief, Subject Cataloging
>   Division. (Published by the Library of
>   Congress.)
> *Main entry:* Haykin, David Judson

Similarly, if a consultant is employed to prepare a study for a corporate body, the name of the consultant becomes the main entry.

> *Title page:*   Library Response to Urban Change, a study
>   of the Chicago Public Library. Lowell A.
>   Martin.
> *Main entry:* Martin, Lowell Arthur

Title as Main Entry

A work whose author is unknown is entered under the title. Anonymous classics and sacred books are included in this category; for a work of this kind a uniform title is used. (See Chapter 5 for the form of heading.)

Examples:

Title page: The Art of Cookery. By a lady.
Main entry: The Art of Cookery
Title page: The Portable Arabian Nights; edited and with an introduction by Joseph Campbell.
Main entry: Arabian Nights
Title page: The Holy Bible, containing the Old and New Testaments; translated out of the original tongues.
Main entry: Bible
Title page: The City and Country Mother Goose. Illustrated by Hilde Hoffman.
Main entry: Mother Goose

When various authors or editors prepare different editions of a work, the main entry is under the title.

Title page: Best Plays of the Year. (Edited in different years by Burns Mantle, John Chapman, and others.)
Main entry: Best Plays of the Year

Almanacs, dictionaries, yearbooks, and periodicals are entered under their titles if the titles are distinctive, and if they are not the work of a personal author. The latter are entered under the author. If the title is not distinctive, entry is under the responsible corporate body.

Examples:

The World Almanac and Book of Facts
The American Heritage Dictionary of the English Language
Yearbook of the American Churches
Better Homes and Gardens

Other Main Entries

There are certain classes of publications which do not fall into any of the preceding categories, e.g., laws, ordinances, constitutions, charters, treaties, liturgical works. Such works are

entered under the appropriate political jurisdictions or church
bodies followed by a form subheading.

Examples:
U.S. *Laws, statutes, etc.*
Richmond, Va. *Ordinances, local laws, etc.*
U.S. *Constitution*
Philadelphia, Pa. *Charter*
U.S. *Treaties, etc.*
Catholic Church. *Liturgy and ritual*

Added Entries 4

An entry, other than a subject, which is made in addition to the main entry for a work is known as an added entry. These entries are made for titles and names not selected as the main entry, for series, and for special or smaller parts of a whole work. Although the main entry is the most important entry for a work, the added entries are necessary because it may be under these terms that a reader seeks the book or other item. Any name, title, or series for which an added entry is made is included in the description of the work; i.e., it appears in the body of the card or in a note.

Title Entries

Title cards are made for most or, in some libraries, all, titles. While the latter practice is automatic and calls for no special decisions, there are instances in which a title card serves no useful purpose, e.g., a work by John Milton whose title is simply *Poems*. However, if the decision to make or not to make a title is going to become time consuming, then it is preferable to make titles for all works cataloged and get on with the rest of the task.

Any part of a title may also be used as an entry if it is felt that a particular word or phrase will be that most likely to be remembered. This is called a "catch title." Thus, a title *The Parable of Sticks and Stones* might well be remembered as "Sticks and Stones"; and so that book might have two title cards, one for the full title and the other for the catch title, "Sticks and Stones." Or, for a title beginning with the author's name, a shortened title (catch title) is made. For instance, a work entitled *Shakespeare's Romeo and Juliet* would have only one title entry, *Romeo and Juliet*.

A former practice was that of using inverted headings; thus the *Parable* title above would have a card under *Sticks and*

Stones, the Parable of. This is awkward, is not actually needed, and can lead to complications; therefore it is no longer recommended.

Sometimes the title of a book and its subject are identical, as in the case of a book entitled *Arithmetic.* It is the policy in some libraries to make the subject card and omit a title card for these works; this can cause trouble later should the subject heading be changed to some other term. It is better to make both subject and title cards when the book is cataloged, because complete access to the book has been provided regardless of any future change which might be made in the subject heading.

See Appendix I for directions for making the title card.

Series Entries

A series entry is made when an individual publication is being cataloged as a complete and separate work but also belongs to a series of importance. The series may be an annual, a monographic series, a publisher's series, or one of several other kinds. (See Figure 6.) If there is likely to be a need for knowing what the library holds in the series or if the series volumes are going to be used or asked for under the series name, an added entry is made carrying the name of the series. Most series are indicated by a note on the unit card following the collation. (See Chapter 6 and Appendix I.)

A series card must be traced on the main entry card for the individual work. This tracing may consist simply of the word "series" or "series: [title of series]." The latter form is used if the book is a part of more than one series.

Restraint should be practiced in making series cards. Entries for publishers' series (e.g., Landmark Books) are rarely made, and there are reference books (such as the *Cumulative Book Index,* publishers' catalogs, and Baer's *Titles in Series*) which supply this information.

Analytics

Parts of some works are of sufficient importance to require cards to bring them out in the catalog. Cards for such entries are called *analytics* since they analyze the contents of the book or set of books.

There are subject analytics, title analytics, author analytics, author-title analytics, and title-author analytics. They are used most often for composite works, collections, compilations, and so forth.

Forman, James
  Ceremony of innocence.   Hawthorn Bks. 1970
249p (A Junior Literary Guild selection)

1 Scholl family—Fiction   2 Germany—Fiction   3 World War, 1939-
1945—Fiction I Title   Fic

Printed cards showing series notes
(no series entries indicated)

Spencer, Herbert, 1820–1903.
    Literary style and music including two short essays on
gracefulness and beauty.   Port Washington, N. Y., Kennikat Press [1970]

    x, 119 p. 19 cm. (Essay and general literature index reprint
series)

    Reprint of the 1951 ed.

1. Style, Literary. 2. Music. 3. Aesthetics.   I. Title.

The Reference shelf   Series entry

378.1   Bander, Edward J   ed.
            Turmoil on the campus.   Wilson, H.W. 1970
        276p (The Reference shelf v42, no.3)

            Educators, representatives of the government, social scientists and political
        observers discuss various aspects of student unrest in the United States and
        the implications of this unrest for the country and for the universities.
        Among the topics covered are causes of the unrest, Black studies, law and
        order, and the events at Kent State University and Jackson State College
            Bibliography : p261-76

        1 Students—U.S.   2 Col-   leges and universities—U.S.   I Title
        II Series   378.1

                                    (W) The H. W. Wilson Company

FIGURE 6

For instance, a group of plays by different authors is bound in
one volume under a collective title. Each play and each author
may be requested; therefore cards are made under the author and
title and, in reverse, under the title and author. For example, for
a volume of plays compiled and edited by Bennett Cerf, each play

should be brought out:

> Sherwood, Robert
>> The petrified forest *author and title analytic*
> Cerf, Bennett, ed.
>> Sixteen famous American plays

> The petrified forest
> Sherwood, Robert *title and author analytic*
> Cerf, Bennett, ed.
>> Sixteen famous American plays

These entries appear above the main entry (compiler, editor, author, or title) of the book.

For a collection of works by one author, we may need a title analytic for each individual work, even though analytics are not needed for the author. His name, of course, is the main entry for the volume.

Example:
> Romeo and Juliet
> Shakespeare, William
>> Shakespeare's tragedies

It is less usual to have author analytics without accompanying titles; but it is possible, for instance, for a collection of speeches or essays, written by different people but with nondistinctive titles.

> Lincoln, Abraham
> Perkins, George, ed.
>> Inaugural addresses of George Washington, Abraham Lincoln, and Woodrow Wilson

(Author analytics would be made for each person.)

Subject analytics will be discussed in Chapter 7.

The decision regarding when and for what works to use analytics depends on such factors as (1) the size and nature of the collection, (2) the amount of material in the library on a subject or by an author, (3) the unusualness of the material, and (4) whether or not the information as to the book's contents is available elsewhere. (For instance, reference books such as the *Essay and General Literature Index*, publications in the Standard Catalog series, and play indexes analyze the contents of many books.) Small libraries generally analyze their materials more than do large ones, since they do not always have so many reference books, and since the reference books (indexes, bibliographies, and so forth) are usually not published until some months or even years later than the books being indexed.

Every analytical card made must be traced on the main entry card for the volume. The tracing may be only the words "auth anals" or "t anals" or "a and t anals," if every author or title listed on the unit card in contents note is used. Or the tracing may say, if necessary, "author anals: Smith, Taylor, Jones," etc. Otherwise the exact tracing for each analytic is listed along with the other tracings. (See Chapter 2 and Appendix I for information on tracings.)

The former practice of including inclusive paging in the analytic entry at the top of the card is no longer recommended. If the exact paging is needed, it is included in the contents note, in a separate note on the unit card, or at the left-hand side of the analytic card below the call number.

　　　　　　　Muskie, Edmund Sixtus, 1914-

815.08　　**Representative** American speeches: 1969-1970; ed. by Lester
R　　　　　　Thonssen. Wilson, H.W. 1970
　　　　　　　208p (The Reference shelf v42, no.4)

p.98-107　This volume, the thirty-third in an annual compilation, contains speeches
　　　　　　by such public figures as President Nixon, Edmund S. Muskie, Glenn T.
　　　　　　Seaborg, and Kenneth B. Clark. The speeches are grouped under the
　　　　　　headings: The continuing agony; Thoughts on broadcast journalism;
　　　　　　National conscience and the environment; and The patterns of change
　　　　　　Biographical notes: p197-203. Cumulative author index: p205-08

　　　　　　1 American orations   2 Speeches, addresses, etc.   ɪ Thonssen, Lester, ed.
　　　　　　ɪɪ Series　　　　　　　　　　　　　　　　　　　　　　　　815.08

　　　　　　　　　　　　　　　　　　　　　　(W) The H. W. Wilson Company

Author analytic on unit card

FIGURE 7

If the contents note is long, requiring several cards, only that card showing the particular item is needed for the analytic. Short-form cards may be made for analytics when unit cards are not used.

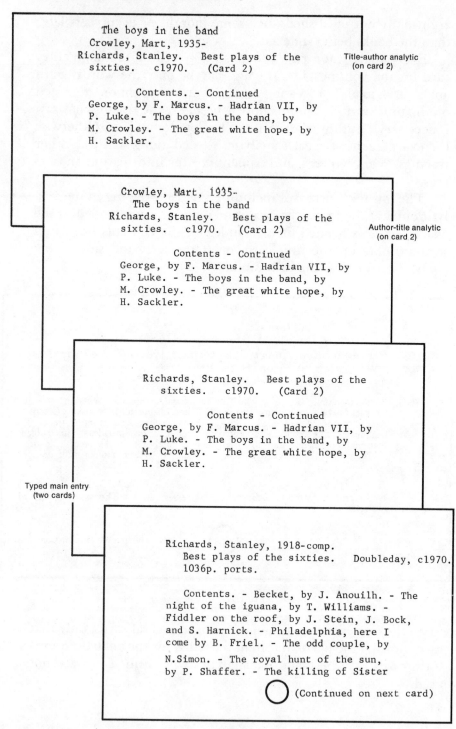

The boys in the band
  Crowley, Mart, 1935-
Richards, Stanley.   Best plays of the
  sixties.   c1970.   (Card 2)

          Title-author analytic
          (on card 2)

        Contents. - Continued
George, by F. Marcus. - Hadrian VII, by
P. Luke. - The boys in the band, by
M. Crowley. - The great white hope, by
H. Sackler.

Crowley, Mart, 1935-
  The boys in the band
Richards, Stanley.   Best plays of the
  sixties.   c1970.   (Card 2)

          Author-title analytic
          (on card 2)

        Contents - Continued
George, by F. Marcus. - Hadrian VII, by
P. Luke. - The boys in the band, by
M. Crowley. - The great white hope, by
H. Sackler.

Richards, Stanley.   Best plays of the
  sixties.   c1970.   (Card 2)

        Contents - Continued
George, by F. Marcus. - Hadrian VII, by
P. Luke. - The boys in the band, by
M. Crowley. - The great white hope, by
H. Sackler.

Typed main entry
(two cards)

Richards, Stanley, 1918-comp.
  Best plays of the sixties.   Doubleday, c1970.
  1036p. ports.

      Contents. - Becket, by J. Anouilh. - The
  night of the iguana, by T. Williams. -
  Fiddler on the roof, by J. Stein, J. Bock,
  and S. Harnick. - Philadelphia, here I
  come by B. Friel. - The odd couple, by
  N.Simon. - The royal hunt of the sun,
  by P. Shaffer. - The killing of Sister

              (Continued on next card)

FIGURE 8

Other Added Entries

If a publication is the joint work of two or three people, the first named, or the one indicated as most responsible for the work, is selected as the main entry; but additional cards are used for the second and third names. These additional entries are known as "joint authors" or "joint editors," as the case may be. The book *Modern Physics*, by Charles E. Dull, H. Clark Metcalfe, and John Williams, would be entered under Charles E. Dull as the main entry, but it would have an added entry for H. Clark Metcalfe as joint author and one for John Williams as joint author. (If more than three people are named, the title is used as main entry, and an added entry is made only for the first name.)

If a work is done for an organization or institution, the author is named as main entry, but the name of the organization or institution, if important to the work, is used as an added entry.

When the main entry for a work is the name of a corporate body, an added entry is made for a personal author, if one is named. If more than one personal author is named, an added entry is made only under the one named first.

Sometimes it is necessary to make an additional card under an illustrator, an editor, the author of an important introduction, a translator, a compiler, or a sponsor—or to show other important relationships to the work. The relationship to the publication, if other than author or joint author, is shown in abbreviated form, such as "ed.," "jt. ed.," "illus." This relationship must also be shown in the description of the book in the body of the card, or in a note on the card, as:

"Critical introduction" by Charles Bradley, p.3-40.

Added entries other than titles should be kept to a minimum. They should not be allowed to multiply just on the off-chance that someone someday might use them, or just because some other library has used them.

5 Form of the Entry

Kinds of Entry

The choice of main and added entries has been discussed in earlier chapters. Not only is it important to select the correct entries, it is also important to follow established practice as to the form in which the entries appear in the catalog. Roughly, the kinds of entries fall into the following categories:

1. The personal name. May be used as main entry, added entry, or subject.
2. The corporate name. May be used as main entry, added entry, or subject.
3. The name of an object. May be used as main entry (though rarely), added entry, or subject.
4. The uniform title. May be used as main entry, added entry, or subject.
5. The real title. May be used as main entry or added entry.
6. The catch title. Used as added entry only.
7. The word as subject (noun). Used only as subject entry.
8. The phrase as subject. Used only as subject entry.

Title entries (5-6) are discussed in Chapters 3 and 4; subject entries (7-8) are taken up in Chapter 7. Guidelines for form of entry for the first four categories are presented in this chapter.

Personal Name

The personal name may be one of several types.

The easiest to work with is the type we are most accustomed to, such as John Clark Jones. This is entered under surname, followed by given name, as: Jones, John Clark. Unfortunately, our mythical Mr. Jones may vary his usage, at one time publishing under his full name, another time under John Jones, another time using J. C. Jones or J. Jones, Clark Jones, J. Clark Jones, or even just Jones or Mr. Jones. There was a time when catalogers did research on every name, exhausting every available source to "establish" the man's full name along with his birth and death dates. Even research libraries have had to give this up as too costly and not justified by need.

The current practice for small libraries is to use the name as it appears on the title page. If the name is the same as one already in a specific catalog for a different person, some distinguishing information is added for the new one. This may be a fuller name or the inclusion of birth and death dates or some other feature. If the person is already in the catalog under a different form of name, the earlier form is used unless there is some pressing reason to prefer the new one. If the newer one is used, it means recataloging all of the materials already cataloged or tying the two forms together through cross references or history cards. (See Appendix I, pages 158-161.)

If a printed card is being used and the name given on it is fuller in form than that given on the title page and it is a name new to the catalog, nothing is gained by cutting it back. If the printed card has a shorter form than that previously used, the additional information can be added to the new cards.

Library of Congress cataloging often uses a name in a form fuller than that on the title page and fuller than that needed for the small library. If the individual library uses LC printed cards, it must decide when it must cut the names back or use a simpler form.

The H. W. Wilson cards now being made use the title-page form of the name in every case, without regard to consistency. In some libraries this may not matter, but others may want to establish one form for each writer so as to keep all his works together. There are good arguments on both sides of this question and the decision—an administrative one—should be made only after careful consideration and with good cause, not just on the basis of what the cataloger is used to doing or used to seeing other libraries do. The strongest argument for each author's having the same form, different from all others, is that it provides for the reader who wants to find all works of an author together. This is necessary in research libraries. The public library patron and, ordinarily, the school library user much more often seek the individual title and find it more easily if the title-page form is used; even if several authors have the same name (e.g., John Smith), the user (who seldom understands the librarian's arbitrarily established items of differentiation) finds the title more easily if all works of all John Smiths are interarranged by title.

Personal names bring other questions and variations, among them: pseudonyms, forenames, changing names, compound names, names with prefixes. In general, the title-page form is used or the form most generally used or best known. But some further comments may be helpful.

A pseudonym is generally preferred, particularly for current and popular material, if it is generally used and known. Books are published, advertised, and sold under the pseudonym, and it is the name used in reviews and discussions. Why make it difficult for the reader to find the book? Public libraries (large and small) have been swinging to the use of pseudonyms for some years, and the schools are also turning in this direction. If an author uses both his real name and a pseudonym, or two or more pseudonyms, each book is entered as its title page indicates. If it is desired, the individual's works may be tied together by means of references or history cards (see Appendix I).

Forenames are used for royalty, popes, saints, members of religious orders, etc. The small library usually has few of their works to worry about; those few can be handled simply by using the name followed by a designation, word, or phrase (in English), to identify him.

Examples:
    Elizabeth II, Queen of Great Britain
    John XXIII, Pope
    Benedict, Saint
    Napoleon I, Emperor of the French
    Margaret, Princess of Great Britain
    Edward, Brother

People sometimes change their names: women marry, people change nationality and language form, etc. Use the name best known (e.g., Pearl Buck) or follow the title page. Following the title page too slavishly may occasionally give trouble since different printings or editions of the same work may be published under different names, but it doesn't happen often enough to weaken the principle.

For compound names or names with prefixes, the practice of the language in which the author writes is observed. Hyphenated names are treated as one name. References from the unused forms are made, if needed.

Examples:
> Fitzmaurice-Kelly, James (reference from Kelly, James Fitzmaurice-)
> FitzGerald, Edward
> De Morgan, Augustus (reference from Morgan, Augustus de)
> Du Maurier, Daphne (reference from Maurier, Daphne du)
> De la Mare, Walter (reference from La Mare, Walter de and from Mare, Walter de la)
> Le Sage, Alain René
> La Fontaine, Jean de
> Goethe, Johann Wolfgang von

Classical writers are entered under the names best known in English, as: Horace, Cicero, Virgil.

Corporate Name

Corporate bodies were discussed as authors in Chapter 3 and as added entries in Chapter 4. The form to be used for a corporate name (other than the names of certain categories of governmental agencies) is that of the title page, or that best known or most used, as:

> American Library Association
> Boy Scouts of America
> Cornell University
> National Aeronautics and Space Administration
> National Underwriter Company
> Tennessee Valley Authority
> Yellowstone National Park

(Note that articles "a" and "the" are not used at the beginning.)

If the name of the corporation is in a foreign language, the English form is used unless the foreign name does not translate well or is extremely well known. Thus:

> National Socialist Party, Germany, *but*
> Bibliothèque Nationale, Paris

If it is necessary to differentiate between two or more institutions or organizations of the same name, the place is added:

> Hawthorne School, Caldwell
> Hawthorne School, Springfield, Ill.
> Hawthorne School, Springfield, Mass.
> First Presbyterian Church, Indianapolis

If a work is produced by a section, chapter, division, or other part of a body, this may be ignored in the entry; the main body is sufficient to identify the work except in very large libraries. Thus, a publication of the Reference Services Division of the American Library Association is entered only under American Library Association. If the division has a distinctive name, the name is used by itself, e.g., American Association of School Librarians (a division of ALA and an associated organization of the National Education Association).

Corporate bodies also include agencies of government. If the agency is one through which a basic legislative, executive, or judicial function of government is exercised, it is entered, in English, as a subdivision under the heading for the governmental jurisdiction.

Examples:
Chicago, Ill. Police Dept.
France. Foreign Office (reference from France. Ministère des Affaires Étrangères)
Great Britain. Parliament
Illinois (State) Dept. of Education
Massachusetts (State) Superior Court
U.S. Dept. of Agriculture

The abbreviation for the state name is used after cities and counties of the United States, and "(State)" is added for states; the name of the country is added for foreign place names. Thus:

Springfield, Ill.
Springfield, Mass.
New York, N.Y.
New York County, N.Y.
New York (State)
Paris, France
Montreal, Canada

These additions serve two purposes: to distinguish two places with the same name and also to differentiate official governmental publications.

Other agencies created and controlled by governments are entered under their names, according to the general rule for the form of entry for corporate bodies.

Library of Congress entries for corporate bodies are most complex, using foreign language forms and many subdivisions; thus these cards are usually unsuitable for the small library. In some cases it is possible to line out the undesired subdivisions, but it is better not to use the cards at all.

Name of Object

Occasionally the name of an object is used (particularly as subject). The best-known form is used, followed by a descriptive word in parentheses if necessary:

    Plymouth Rock
    Leaning Tower of Pisa
    Eiffel Tower
    Liberty Bell (Ship)
    U.S.S. Constitution (Ship)

Form Headings

For some entries extremely vague or variable in form, stylized forms have been established. The following types of publications are covered by this category of heading: Laws, Ordinances, Constitutions, Charters, Treaties, and Liturgical Works. These are entered under the appropriate jurisdiction, followed by the form heading, as:

    Pennsylvania (State) *Laws, statutes, etc.*
    Baltimore, Md. *Ordinances, local laws, etc.*
    Australia. *Constitution*
    Chicago, Ill. *Charter*
    U.S. Treaties, *etc.*
    Church of England. *Liturgy and ritual*

Uniform Titles

Some works ("classics," epics, folk stories, etc.) have come down to us through the ages and have no known authors; or they are derived from cycles of tales and are published under various titles. These include Mother Goose, the Pearl, Reynard the Fox, the Song of Roland, the Arabian Nights, Beowulf, the Fall of the Nibelungen, the Book of the Dead, Cynewulf, etc. For these, the English form is used with "see" references from well-known titles in foreign languages, as illustrated in Figure 9.

In some cases, an author is identified with groups of folk or epic stories even though these stories also exist separately. Best known of these are (1) the stories of Arthur and the Knights of the Round Table, which may or may not stem from the writings of Malory, and (2) Aesop's fables. If the book is definitely identified as the work of one man, his name is used as author; otherwise the standard name is used, as:

    Aesop
    King Arthur

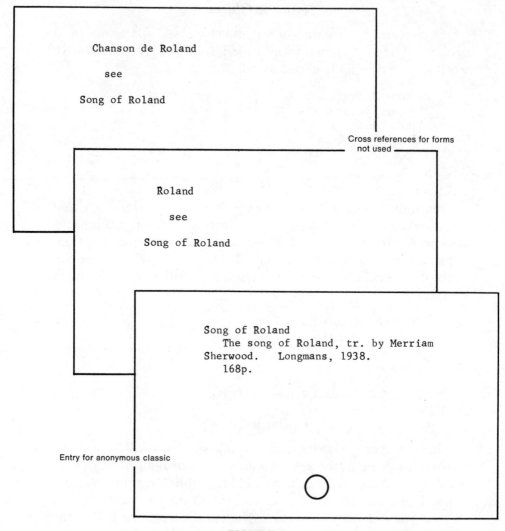

```
    Chanson de Roland

        see

    Song of Roland
```

Cross references for forms not used

```
        Roland

          see

    Song of Roland
```

```
    Song of Roland
        The song of Roland, tr. by Merriam
    Sherwood.    Longmans, 1938.
        168p.
```

Entry for anonymous classic

FIGURE 9

Even works of known authors may appear under many titles. *Don Quixote,* for instance, in addition to all its editions in Spanish and other languages, has been published in English under the titles *The History of the Valorous and Witty Knight-Errant, Don-Quixote of the Mancha; The Life and Exploits of the Ingenious Gentleman Don Quixote de la Mancha; The History of the Renowned Don Quixote de la Mancha; Don Quixote de la Mancha; The Adventures of Don Quixote; The History of the Ingenious Gentleman; The Ingenious Gentleman Don Quixote de la Mancha,* and many more.

If the library has several editions of such a work, it is easiest to adopt one form and use it at the beginning of the title, in brackets to show it does not appear on the title page. (This is one of the few times the use of brackets is recommended.) This device should not be used unless the library has several editions of the title or there is good reason to think it will have many and that following the title pages would result in the editions' being separated.

Example:
    Cervantes Saavedra, Miguel de
        [Don Quixote]
        The adventures of Don Quixote . . .

In this case, instead of making title references for unused forms or title cards for each form, one title reference is made, reading:

        Don Quixote
    Cervantes Saavedra, Miguel de
        For all editions of this work see entries under author

Form titles may also be used to bring together collected works of a prolific author. For instance, the library may have several books by Shakespeare with titles beginning with such phrases as "Complete Works," "Shakespeare's Tragedies," "Plays," "Four Comedies," etc. For these the form title "Works" will bring the titles together in one place without leaving interpretation and decision to the filer in such directives as, "File all collected works of an author together followed by titles of individual works." The entry looks like this:

    Shakespeare, William
        [Works]
        Complete works

In this case no title cards or title references are needed.

In a large library entries under the Bible are quite detailed because of the number of versions, parts, languages, and editions in its collection. However, the small library will have relatively few editions and versions, so a simple rule suffices. Enter the Bible and any of its parts under the uniform title "Bible." Add to the uniform title the designation of the parts, as:

    Bible.
    Bible. O.T.
    Bible. O.T. Apocrypha
    Bible. N.T. Luke

6 Descriptive Cataloging

The term *cataloging* is sometimes employed inclusively to cover all of the activities involved in organizing library materials. It is also the term used for any specific part of the work such as establishing the form of entry. Catalogers themselves most often speak of cataloging in relation to its professional aspects as distinguished from the administrative and clerical ones of implementation. The professional work may be divided into two parts: (1) descriptive cataloging, which includes establishing the entries (main and added entries), both as to choice and form, and the descriptive information carried on the cards; (2) subject cataloging, which includes assigning classification numbers and subject headings to material.

This may be shown in outline form:

Cataloging in Its Broadest Sense

I. Administration of the catalog work
   A. Establishing goals of service
   B. Planning and establishing procedures and flow of work
   C. Selecting and providing care for supplies and equipment
   D. Supervising personnel, including assignments of tasks
   E. Coordinating cataloging with the other library activities
   F. Maintaining the catalog or catalogs.
      1. Acquiring and/or making cards
      2. Filing cards
      3. Arranging for number and kinds of catalogs
      4. Providing aids for catalog use
      5. Keeping catalog or catalogs up to date
   G. Shelf-listing and maintaining the shelf list

H. Physically preparing the materials
    I. Maintaining statistics and making reports

II. Professional cataloging
    A. Descriptive cataloging
        1. Choosing entries
            a. Main entries
            b. Added entries
        2. Establishing form of entries
        3. Selecting descriptive information carried on the card
        4. Arranging information on the card
    B. Subject cataloging
        1. Assigning subject classification numbers (or call numbers)
        2. Selecting subject headings

This chapter deals with parts 3 and 4 of II A of the outline.

Information on the Catalog Card

The items of information, any of which may appear on a full unit catalog card, include:

1. The call number
    a. Location symbol or designation
    b. Subject classification number
    c. Letter for main entry (author's surname, first word of corporate entry, or first word—not an article—of the title)
    d. Cutter number
    e. Work letter
    f. Edition designation (number or date)
    g. Volume or publication number

2. The main entry
    a. Personal name
    b. Corporate name
    c. Uniform heading
    d. Title

3. The title statement
    a. Form title
    b. Main title
    c. Subtitle or alternate title
    d. "By" statement

    e. Statement of joint responsibility
      (1) Joint author
      (2) Joint editor
      (3) Editor
      (4) Translator
      (5) Illustrator
      (6) Sponsoring or collaborating body
    f. Edition statement

4. Imprint
    a. Place of publication
    b. Publisher's name
    c. Date of publication (or copyright date)

5. Collation
    a. Paging or volume numbering
    b. Size
    c. Illustrative information

6. Series note

7. Other notes
    a. Bibliography
    b. Contents
    c. Publication history
    d. Relation of work to other works
    e. Annotation
    f. Other explanatory information

8. Tracings
    a. For subjects (designated by arabic numerals or capital letters)
    b. For other added entries (designated in entry form or by roman numerals)
      (1) Joint author or other joint responsibility
      (2) Sponsoring or collaborating body
      (3) Titles

No library includes all of this information on any one card; small libraries never use all of it, and what they do use is in an abbreviated form.

Arrangement of Information

The title page forms the basis for the description, but it need not be followed closely. (We are cataloging the book, not the title page.) Unnecessary information is eliminated, items used in the description do not always follow their order on the title page, and some information may be supplied. Omitted or transposed information is no longer indicated by the use of three dots. The *Anglo-American Cataloging Rules* specify that information in the descriptive paragraph supplied from a source other than the title page be enclosed in brackets. In a catalog of the size and nature for which this manual is intended, this use of brackets is unnecessary.

There is an accepted order for arranging the information on the card. Other things being equal, it is well to follow the form, but rigid conformity is no longer considered essential. The placement is indicated by (1) the left-hand edge of the card, (2) the "first indention," (3) the "second indention," etc. (see Appendix I for spacing).

On the main entry line (which is the top line of the main entry or unit card) the following items appear, reading from left to right: the classification number, the author's name, and his birth and death dates, if used. If the main entry is an editor or illustrator, etc., the relationship is shown after the name or dates, for example, "ed." or "illus." One line below the author or main entry and at the second indention begins the title, which is generally taken from the title page of the book. It is in paragraph form if more than one line is required. If a uniform title (see pages 51-53) is used, it appears one line below the author at second indention, and the title page title drops to the next line, second indention. The title includes the "by" phrase if, for any reason, the author statement differs from the name used as the main entry. Among the differences to be brought out on the card is joint or multiple authorship. Not more than three names are given, the rest being indicated by "and others." The title transcription also includes information about the edition, and any information necessary to distinguish the work from others.

Following the title transcription, in the same paragraph, is the imprint: place of publication, publisher's name, and date. The place is not necessary for general publishers, nor for publishers in New York, nor at all in the case of small libraries; if used, only the first-mentioned place is named. The publisher's name is shortened to the prominent name ("Scribner," "Little, Brown"). The date preferred is the copyright date (usually found on the back—or "verso"—of the title page). A small "c" precedes the copyright date. If no copyright date is shown, the imprint (title page) date is used. Fiction and children's books may not need any date (see page 64), or the earliest publishing date may be used. If that date is old (as for standard works), a note may be added: "First published 1878," etc.

Below the title paragraph come the collation (paging, illustrative matter, size) and the series note. If collation is included (and it is recommended for nonfiction though not for fiction or for children's picture books), it is restricted to the last arabic numeral printed in the book's paging and to the word "illus." or "map" for any illustrative material. Size is not noted. If Library of Congress cards are used, the size (or any of the above information) may be left on the cards even though it is not noted on typed or other locally prepared cards.

If the book is part of a series, that information follows the collation or is located where the collation would be and is enclosed in parentheses.

Bibliographic information or other notes follow in lines below, each note being a separate paragraph. Notes may call attention to a distinctive feature of the book; list the contents; or give information relating the book to others, indicating, for example, a change of title or a sequence. Wilson cards carry annotations (brief, noncritical descriptions of the content and coverage of the works), and this practice is being adopted by some schools and public libraries. The Library of Congress now provides annotations on its cards for children's books. (For examples of contents notes see Appendix I.)

Figure 10 illustrates a typed catalog card, with the parts indicated.

If there is no author and the work is entered under the title, a "hanging indention" is used; that is, the title starts at the first indention on the top line, and the full title transcription and imprint all stay within the second indention. (See Figure 11.)

Some libraries and processing centers photograph the LC cataloging information supplied in the *Publishers Weekly* and the *American Book Publishing Record* and enlarge it. This information is arranged in the customary order but is grouped in one paragraph, with the different elements shown in different type faces.

Books in Series

Published works often have direct relationships to other published works. These relationships may be in the form of books in series, sequels, sets of books, serials (including periodicals) and

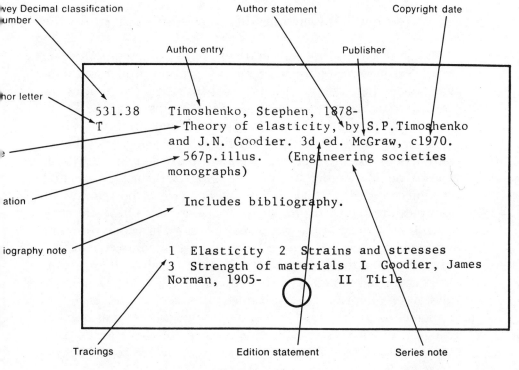

Dewey Decimal classification number

Author entry

Author statement

Publisher

Copyright date

Author letter

e

531.38
T

Timoshenko, Stephen, 1878-
Theory of elasticity, by S.P.Timoshenko
and J.N. Goodier. 3d ed. McGraw, c1970.
567p.illus.   (Engineering societies
monographs)

collation

Includes bibliography.

bibliography note

1 Elasticity   2 Strains and stresses
3 Strength of materials   I Goodier, James
Norman, 1905-   II Title

Tracings

Edition statement

Series note

FIGURE 10

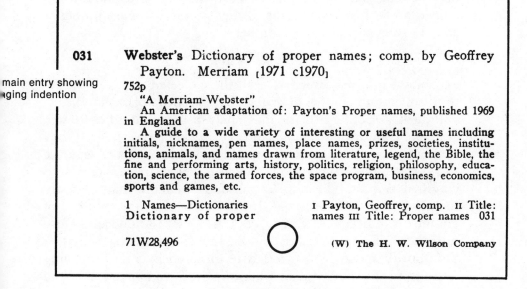

031

main entry showing
hanging indention

Webster's Dictionary of proper names; comp. by Geoffrey
    Payton. Merriam [1971 c1970]
752p
    "A Merriam-Webster"
    An American adaptation of: Payton's Proper names, published 1969
in England
    A guide to a wide variety of interesting or useful names including
initials, nicknames, pen names, place names, prizes, societies, institutions, animals, and names drawn from literature, legend, the Bible, the
fine and performing arts, history, politics, religion, philosophy, education, science, the armed forces, the space program, business, economics,
sports and games, etc.

1 Names—Dictionaries   I Payton, Geoffrey, comp. II Title:
Dictionary of proper   names III Title: Proper names 031

71W28,496   (W) The H. W. Wilson Company

FIGURE 11

variant editions. It is sometimes difficult to distinguish among the types.

Books in series follow one another in progression or sequence, or are closely related in content, and are grouped under an inclusive name. There are publishers' series (usually a group of books planned to meet a certain demand or age level) such as the Landmark Books or the Little Golden Books. There are information books or texts which progress in difficulty, such as numbered arithmetic books or readers; these are usually designated by volume or "book" number, or by grade. There are true series related by subject and/or format which may or may not be numbered; examples are The Chronicles of America and The Reference Shelf. Lastly, there are works (usually fiction) in which the story and the characters are carried from volume to volume, as in the Jalna books or the Babar stories. Books in such series are generally cataloged separately but tied together by a series note. If the series is important, a series added entry is made (see page 41).

Some works are issued as sequels to other works, or as parts of trilogies. When these publications lack a collective series title, "Followed by" and "Preceded by" notes are added to the appropriate cards.

If the volumes of a series are numbered and they are classified as a set (see below) with a common call number, each volume may be separately cataloged. In that case, the series note is included on each set of cards, and the specific volume number is added to the common call number.

Books in Sets

Some works are issued in sets: the collected works of an author, collections of types of materials, reference works, etc. If each volume is a separate title (such as a play or novel), it is best to separate the volumes and catalog and classify them separately. If they cannot be broken up, as in the case of an encyclopedia or separate works continued from volume to volume, they are cataloged and classified as a set. The publication dates (if more than one) are inclusive (e.g., 1950-55), and, instead of paging, the number of volumes is indicated (3 v., 2 v., etc.). If the set is cataloged before publication is completed, it is done as an "open entry"; that is, the imprint shows the earliest date followed by a dash, leaving space to fill in the last date when the set is completed, and the collation shows just "—v." with space for completion.

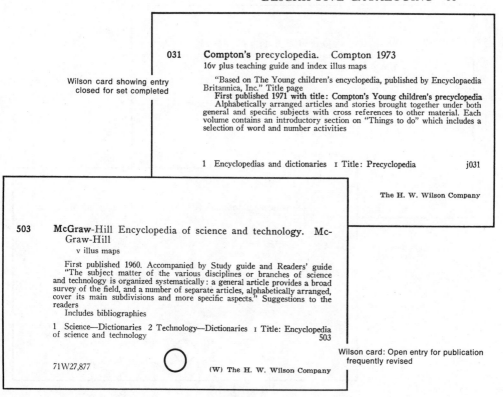

031   **Compton's** precyclopedia.   Compton 1973
16v plus teaching guide and index illus maps

Wilson card showing entry
closed for set completed

"Based on The Young children's encyclopedia, published by Encyclopaedia Britannica, Inc." Title page
First published 1971 with title: Compton's Young children's precyclopedia
Alphabetically arranged articles and stories brought together under both general and specific subjects with cross references to other material. Each volume contains an introductory section on "Things to do" which includes a selection of word and number activities

1 Encyclopedias and dictionaries i Title: Precyclopedia   j031

The H. W. Wilson Company

503   **McGraw**-Hill Encyclopedia of science and technology.   McGraw-Hill
v illus maps

First published 1960. Accompanied by Study guide and Readers' guide
"The subject matter of the various disciplines or branches of science and technology is organized systematically: a general article provides a broad survey of the field, and a number of separate articles, alphabetically arranged, cover its main subdivisions and more specific aspects." Suggestions to the readers
Includes bibliographies

1 Science—Dictionaries 2 Technology—Dictionaries i Title: Encyclopedia of science and technology   503

71W27,877   (W) The H. W. Wilson Company

Wilson card: Open entry for publication frequently revised

FIGURE 12

Serials, Including Periodicals

In the *Anglo-American Cataloging Rules* a serial is defined as "a publication issued in successive parts bearing numerical or chronological designations and intended to be continued indefinitely." Serials include such materials as periodicals, reports, yearbooks, memoirs, proceedings, bulletins, and transactions. The small library has few of these and seldom catalogs those it has—periodicals, almost never. A few rules are sufficient for this type of material (see Chapter 14).

A serial is entered under the title, with hanging indention and, if incomplete, with an open entry (see above, under Books in Sets). If the serial is ended or completed, the cataloging is closed; that is, the concluding dates are indicated and the total number of volumes given. If the publication changes title, each part is cataloged under the title at time of publication, and the records of parts are brought together on the catalog cards by means of notes: "Preceded by . . ." and "Continued as . . . ."

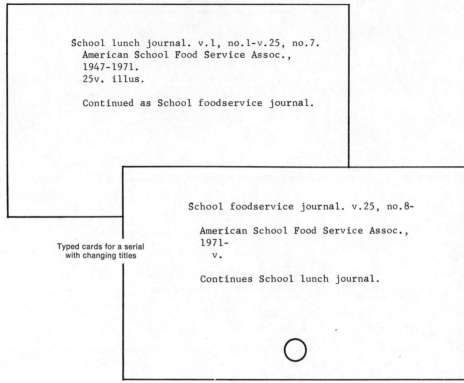

School lunch journal. v.1, no.1-v.25, no.7.
   American School Food Service Assoc.,
   1947-1971.
   25v. illus.

Continued as School foodservice journal.

Typed cards for a serial
with changing titles

School foodservice journal. v.25, no.8-

   American School Food Service Assoc.,
   1971-
   v.

Continues School lunch journal.

FIGURE 13

Variant Editions

Generally a new edition of a book is cataloged separately if it varies in content from the preceding one. Some works are frequently revised or issued at frequent intervals with different contents (such as almanacs, yearbooks, "Best plays," etc.); public and school libraries find it helpful to catalog these as open entries (like true serials), thus avoiding much recataloging. In research libraries many more editions of works are retained, and details of edition variation are important. For this reason those LC cards which catalog each edition separately are not usually followed by small libraries.

Different editions of a work may sometimes be published under different titles. These should be cataloged under the title page for version (or versions) in the library, variations being indicated with a note: "Published also under the title . . . ," "Published in . . . as . . . ," or "Translation of . . . ." If published under many different titles, the work should be entered under a uniform title (see pages 51-53).

The World almanac and book of facts. <s>1886</s>-1972
   New York world telegram, etc., <s>1886</s>-1968-72
   5v. illus.

   Title varies slightly.

Card for title frequently revised
(minor title changes)

FIGURE 14

Fiction and Children's Picture Books

For nonfiction (adult or juvenile) more information is needed about the work than for fiction. For factual material, the edition, the editor, the publisher, the publication date, and the paging are important as showing the age of the information, the authority, etc. Since the cataloging is exact, a separate set of catalog cards is required for each edition or version except for the frequently revised works noted in the section above.

jF   Alcott, Louisa May, 1832-1888
           Jack and Jill. first pub. 1868.

Shelf-list entry for title showing the
date of original publication

FIGURE 15

Fiction and children's picture (or "easy") books do not require such exact identification; in fact, all that is required is the name of the author, a short title, and the copyright date. For older, standard fiction, the date may be omitted, or the note "first pub. . . ." may be used (see Figure 15). Thus one cataloging will take care of all printings and editions of a work of this type. This method of handling the material saves much time since fiction and picture books have the heaviest duplication and discard pattern.

If the name of the illustrator is important (as it sometimes is in identifying different editions of children's books), this information may be indicated on the shelf-list card, relating it to the individual copies. (See Chapter 10.)

Subject Cataloging 7

Subject Entries

As indicated in Chapter 2, one of the important reference services of the catalog is to show what material the library has on different subjects. Classification locates the book by subject, but each book can stand in only one place, and subject entries in the catalog bring out other subject facets, and also relate subjects to one another and suggest new approaches. Even the tracings are helpful in this. Specialists may often seek a specific book under author or title entry, but students and laymen (and even specialists are laymen in all but their own specialties) lean heavily on the subject approach.

Subjects are shown by the use of names, words, or phrases as filing terms or entries. These are added (one card for each subject entry) in capital letters at the top of the unit card. (Formerly subjects were typed in red, but in the present age of rapid copying machines, printing, and photographic copying of cards, red is no longer practical.)

Any person—real, mythological, or fictional—may be a subject. The form for his name is the same as that for an author. Any object, institution, organization, or governmental or other body can become a subject for discussion or study; here again the form follows that of the other entries.

Words and phrases, however, are so varied in form and arrangement and their meanings so overlapping, that special guidance is needed to insure uniformity and consistency. For this reason, lists of subject headings have been prepared, and a selected one is followed. There are literally dozens of these lists, most for use with certain subject fields or specialties such as medicine, aeronautics, music, and law. The school library and the public library, however, need consider only the general lists.

Lists of Headings

The largest and fullest of these is *Subject Headings Used in the Dictionary Catalogs of the Library of Congress*. Designed for use in cataloging collections running into the millions, this list is not needed for children's books or for school libraries (with the possible exception of large technical or college preparatory high schools.) Larger public libraries use LC subjects for adult books, but smaller ones do not need them. These subjects are the ones indicated on LC cards. The small library using LC cards may find that it must use shorter, simpler, or more general terms and will therefore not follow all LC suggestions for subjects.

Sears List of Subject Headings, revised by Barbara M. Westby, is recommended for use in those libraries for which this cataloging manual is intended. The list is designed on the same principles and follows in general the practices of the LC list; the two can be used to supplement each other, with some alteration when necessary. Sears is revised every five or six years, with emphasis on the updating of terminology and the inclusion of headings for new concepts. Sears headings, moreover, are used on Wilson cards. Before using the Sears list, the cataloger should study carefully both the preface and the introductory section, Subject Headings: Principles and Applications of the Sears List (10th ed., 1972); in addition to presenting information on the use of the list, it gives a brief course in subject cataloging.

For children's books, Elva Smith's *Subject Headings for Children's Materials* was very good at one time but has been out of print and out of date for many years. If the subject headings in a children's catalog were taken originally from the Smith list, they can be supplemented by headings from Sears; if this is done, great care must be taken in the making of cross references (see pages 67-68).

In 1952 the ALA published *Subject Headings for Children's Materials*, by Eloise Rue and Effie LaPlante, which was designed especially for school libraries, observing the philosophy of the educational institution. This, too, has become dated, and at present there are no plans for revising it. Moreover, it is difficult to use it in conjunction with other lists, since it reverses in some places the principles followed by LC, Smith, and Sears. The tenth edition of Sears incorporates those headings from LC's *Subject Headings for Children's Literature* which were not already standard headings in the Sears list. This, plus the degree of sophistication of today's children, makes dependence on a separate list of headings for children's cataloging unnecessary.

It has sometimes been argued that school libraries should use terminology which follows the curriculum. This is not recommended by experienced librarians since it confuses the child who has to use different libraries. It is better to make references from educational terms to equivalent headings in the list being used.

Structure and Use of a Subject Heading List

A list of subject headings is really a network of subject entries and cross references. Such a list contains general subjects, specific subjects, divisions of subjects, cross references from subjects not used, references from one subject to related subjects, and notes indicating the scope of a subject.

A subject entry may be a noun, two nouns joined by "and," a phrase, or a noun and an adjective — for example:

EDUCATION
EDUCATION AND STATE
EDUCATION OF PRISONERS
EDUCATION, ELEMENTARY

Subject headings may be subdivided to show the form of a work, an aspect of a subject, the geographic area with which the book is concerned, and the period of time covered by the work:

CHEMISTRY–DICTIONARIES
ARCHITECTURE–DETAILS
LIBRARIES–U.S.
U.S.–HISTORY–1919-1933

A requisite of a subject heading list is the inclusion of references. These are of two kinds: (1) *See* references from terms not used to terms in the list, and (2) *See also* references from one subject to related subjects, or from a general to a more specific subject:

EDUCATION, CHRISTIAN
see
RELIGIOUS EDUCATION

CONSTITUTIONS, STATE
see also
STATE GOVERNMENTS

ARCHITECTURE–DESIGNS AND PLANS
see also
ARCHITECTURE, DOMESTIC–DESIGNS AND PLANS

When a subject heading is selected from the list of subject headings, it is not necessary to make all of the references included in the list; in fact, a *see also* reference is never made unless the subject referred to appears in the catalog.

It is absolutely necessary to keep a record of all subject headings used and of all references made. This can be done by maintaining a subject authority file on 3 x 5 cards, but it is simpler to check entries in the list as they are used. If subject headings from an additional source are used, these must be written in the subject heading list. When the last card under a heading is withdrawn, records must be corrected. (See Chapter 15.)

Technique of Subject Cataloging

Subject cataloging is perhaps the most important aspect of cataloging, because much of a library's materials are requested by subject. The cataloger must be able to determine the subject or subjects treated by the author. Just as there is a procedure to follow in performing the descriptive cataloging, so there is one for subject cataloging.

The cataloger notes the title and subtitle, reads the preface or introduction, and reads through the table of contents. It is frequently necessary to skim through the text in order to determine the subject of the work. Chapter summaries and final summaries are helpful to the cataloger. If the subject is one with which the cataloger is not acquainted, help may be sought from encyclopedias or other reference works. When the subject has been determined, the proper term to express it is then selected from the list of subject headings.

A subject card is made if an entire work is about one subject or if a major part or section of a book is about one subject. To bring out different facets or relationships, several subject entries are sometimes needed. The number used depends on the complexity and importance of the book, the size and goals of the library, and the amount of material available on the subject. A small library will make more subject entries on general topics than will a large one; the larger one may be more interested in bringing out a new or little-known topic of interest to only a few specialists. The beginning cataloger tends to make too many subject entries. He should not try to analyze every thought in the book but should deal only with its major contributions. Subjects go out of date quickly, in both terminology and concepts, and the cataloger who is overgenerous in assigning them only makes re-cataloging more difficult.

Analytics

Subject analytics may be used for parts of a collection or even for a section of a single work. Thus a collection of biographies may have names as subjects; or a book may have a separate section on a subject.

ART, FRENCH
Johnson, Harold
Modern European painting

GLENN, JOHN
Smith, James E.
The astronauts

A collection of essays or a book consisting of parts written by different authors may require subject analytics. It may also need author analytics. It could conceivably have all three: author, subject, and title analytics.

Any book which has a separate part or a noteworthy section of many pages devoted to a subject different from the subject used for the entire book may need a subject analytic.

Subject Headings and Regional Processing

It is in subject work that a cooperative or regional processing center is most helpful; but, paradoxically, it is in subject work that the center leaves most work to be done in the individual library. The centralized work is helpful because it is done by experienced people who have adequate tools available, and also because the work is suitable (assuming that the cooperative venture comprises libraries of comparable sizes and goals). But subject cards, even from these centers, must be consistent with those in the individual catalog and must be reinforced by the proper references. Ideally, perhaps, the cataloger from the center visits the cooperating libraries to advise and check on the work. In a school system, the communication can be much closer and more uniform than in public libraries located in different towns. But even a large public library system in a single city finds it difficult to keep branch catalogs up to date and accurate, so the problem is always present.

Subject work is most important and most difficult, calling for a wide background of information and knowledge and also for judgment. It cannot be done thoughtlessly or slapdash or turned over to a typist. It requires careful study of methods and principles, complete comprehension of the information contained in the introductory material of the list employed, careful study of each publication, and thoughtful consideration of the work in relation to the library's collections, clientele, and goals. Nor may a subject, once selected, be forgotten; each new book or new term calls for reevaluation of older usage, possibly for recataloging.

Classification of Books 8

As noted in Chapter 2, most books in the collection require some classification in order to lead the user from the card catalog to a specific subject, and also to group together the books on the same or related subjects.

Classification Schemes

If there are only a few appropriate lists of subject headings, there is even less choice for the classification scheme or schedule to be followed. Only two general classification schemes are widely used in America today: the Library of Congress classification (LC) and the Dewey Decimal classification (DC).

The Library of Congress classification is composed of letters and numbers, utilizing twenty-one letters of the alphabet for its main classes. The combination of letters and numbers allows for provision of great specificity in classification without producing a class number of fifteen or more digits. LC is an excellent classification for very large libraries or for special or research libraries where there is a concentration of many books in a subject area, but it shouldn't be considered for school or small public libraries.

The Dewey Decimal classification is the overwhelming choice for schools and public libraries and should be adequate for most church libraries. (A genuine research collection of theological materials would do better with LC, however.) Dewey is the classification most used in general libraries and best known to library users. It is also followed by many printed bibliographies and library tools, both in arrangement and in indicating classification numbers for individual titles. Its Relative Index and its mnemonic features (certain numbers carrying the same meaning throughout) make it easy to learn and to use. But perhaps its strongest point is its adaptability to the size and nature of a collection.

Dewey Classification

Dewey divides all knowledge into nine subject classes (100-900) with a tenth (000) for general materials. Each class number is subdivided by 10, these 10 again by 10, and then each whole number by decimals for specific breakdowns. The structure allows the individual library to classify as broadly or as specifically as its collections and purposes demand. This feature is reflected in the Dewey publishing pattern; there is a full edition and an abridged one for libraries up to 20,000 titles. Each starts with summary tables. While it is possible to assign to certain books classification numbers of seventeen or more digits, each representing a refinement, it is just as correct to use, when appropriate, a much shorter number for the same book. Elementary schools and very small public libraries will seldom if ever need to go beyond three or four digits. Larger high schools and medium-sized public libraries may need to expand in certain subjects to four or five figures (one or two beyond the decimal point) and in a few subjects even to six figures. The abridged edition is adequate for small libraries; it expands where expansion is needed and is the safest guide to follow.

The ten classes of Dewey are as follows:

000	General works
100	Philosophy
200	Religion
300	Social sciences
400	Language
500	Pure science
600	Technology
700	The arts
800	Literature
900	History

One subject may be traced through its steps, with intervening numbers omitted, to illustrate flexibility:

```
600   Technology
  620   Engineering and allied operations
    621   Applied physics
      621.3   Electrical, electronic and electromagnetic engineer-
                ing
        621.38   Electronic and communication engineering
          621.384   Radio and radar engineering
            621.3848   Radar
```

Thus a book on radar engineering might be classed in any one of these seven numbers depending on the size of the collection and the degree of specificity needed. If the library has twenty or thirty books in its entire technology group, all engineering books could be put in the general engineering number 620; if it had a large collection on engineering, the seven digits might be employed, thus locating the book on radar in its precise slot.

For the inexperienced classifier the danger is in being too specific. It is wasted effort and only confusing to use the most specific (longest) number for each book in a small collection. The numbers on Wilson cards are safe to follow. The suggested Dewey numbers on Library of Congress cards usually need to be shortened. The classifiers at LC deliberately carry numbers to the farthest possible subdivision, taking it for granted that individual libraries will cut them to suit their needs.

Fiction, Juvenile Books, and Other Variations

Simpler and shorter numbers can be used for children's books than for those in adult collections since there is much less material available in each subject field. And certain kinds of materials for either adults or children can be given group designations. "F" has been used in many libraries for fiction and "B" or 92 for individual biography. "Easy" or picture books can also be grouped under a single symbol such as "E." Or, preferably, fiction, at least fiction in English, is not classed at all, but simply shelved in a separate, author-arranged collection. In this case, it has been found helpful to have the word "Fiction" appear on the catalog cards where the classification number usually appears—since the users have been instructed to get a "number," they sometimes select any item on the card if the call number space is blank.

A public library or church library needs to differentiate between adult and juvenile materials and uses a small "j" before the class number for children's books, as j530, jB, jF. Public libraries usually classify a title which appears in both adult and juvenile collections with the same number, but some compromise may occasionally be necessary for certain types of material. Children's librarians, for instance, may want to classify fictionalized biography with biography, whereas librarians working with adults treat it as fiction. Legends, folk stories, and fairy stories may be made a separate collection in the children's room or kept with fiction; in the adult collection they may be classified as folklore. Titles which go only into the children's collection can, of course, be classified as simply as possible and in the class where they are the most useful in work with children.

Classifying a Book

A manual to explain the Library of Congress application of Dewey numbers is available, but small libraries will find the introduction to the abridged edition of the Dewey Decimal classification scheme an adequate preparation; a careful reading of it is essential before any attempt is made to classify.

Classification is a third area, along with establishing the main entry and subject cataloging, which calls for knowledge, experience, and judgment. The cataloger must study the book being classified, the classification scheme, and the individual library's collection. He must class each book in relation to what has been done before but must also face a world in which knowledge is growing and changing at a dizzy pace.

A book can stand in only one place on the shelf, so it has only one classification number. If a book treats of more than one subject or several aspects of a subject, the cataloger assigns subject headings for the additional topics treated by the author (see Chapter 7).

The cataloger can find classification assistance available from printed cards and from such tools as the Wilson Standard Catalog series, *The Booklist*, *Publishers Weekly*, and *Book Review Digest* —all of which give suggested classifications.

Call Numbers and Cutter Numbers

A call number is a number assigned to a book to distinguish it from others. It got this name because in former days books were kept in stacks or shelves inaccessible to the public, and the patron requested or "called for" the book he had selected by means of the catalog. This is still true, of course, of any part of the collection which is closed to the reader.

A full call number may include a subject classification number; a letter or letters plus a number representing the author's name; a "book" or "work" letter indicating the title; and designations as needed for edition, volume or copy number, special location symbol, and size indication. Thus, an arithmetic book entitled *Playing with Numbers*, by Becker, might have a number like

511
B39p3
v.2

This shows that the book is on arithmetic (511) and will be shelved with other arithmetic books. The author number (B39) is obtained by combining the initial letter of the author's last name with a number from a numerical table so designed as to insure, through its use, an alphabetical arrangement. This is also called a Cutter number since the tables were devised by C. A. Cutter; they were later expanded from two to three figures by Kate Sanborn and are called the Cutter-Sanborn tables. For most names, one initial and two numbers are used; for names beginning with vowels or S, two letters and one number are needed, thus: Sm5, An3.

The "p" in the Becker call number derives from the title, and the 3 following shows it to be the third edition of this work. A third line is required for a work of two or more volumes. The call numbers on the catalog cards do not, as a general rule, include volume numbers, since the cards apply to all volumes of the set. The volume number does appear on the back (spine) of the book, on the book card, and on the book pocket.

Not all of this call number is needed for the small public library, still less for the school or church library. The usual practice is to use just an initial for the author, thus:

511
B

The book is then shelved with other books with the same classification number, alphabetically by the author's name (except for biography, described below). This sometimes means lettering the author's name on the spine of the book, if it does not already appear there or if the name printed is not the one used in cataloging.

How large a library should be before it considers the use of Cutter numbers is a question debated among librarians. If there are so many books in one class as to make shelving or finding individual titles difficult, there are two ways to break up the group: closer (more exact) classification or the use of Cutter numbers. Generally, the first is preferable since it can be employed only where needed.

A second reason for considering the use of Cutter numbers is the need for differentiation among various editions of a work. Each edition of a nonfiction book requires separate cataloging; if multiple editions of a title are kept, the need arises to differentiate. This may be done by using a full call number or by making the publication date part of the number, thus:

511
T
1963

Some librarians use Cutter numbers only for the more crowded classes of material, such as 398.2 (legends) or biography, and use just initials elsewhere.

Whether classified (in 920-929), kept in 92, or B, individual biography is cataloged by author but arranged according to biographee. If a Cutter number is used, it is the number for the subject, and it is followed by a letter for the author, with a second letter, if needed, for the title. Thus, Sloane's life of Robinson is

B
R65s

If Sloane writes a second book on Robinson, another letter is added after the "s," as "sl." If there are biographies on other Robinsons, different numbers are used, as: R651, R652.

Special Markings or Symbols

Size creates a need for another symbol in libraries in which very large or very small books are separately shelved. Such shelving saves space, for shelves can be placed nine or ten inches apart to accommodate most books. Very small books (under three inches in height) are not shelved in place because they are too easily lost or mislaid. The few small books may be kept in a drawer or cupboard and the catalog and shelf-list cards stamped "Shelved separately. Ask at desk." Books too large for standard shelving can be shelved, according to number, in a special section with high shelves. (They should never be turned on their fore-edges, as this practice breaks the backs.) For these a "q" may precede the class number (q759) on all cards and on the book itself. The letter stands for "quarto," a term adapted from the rare book trade and in general usage. Some libraries even have groupings by size, e.g., those up to nine inches, those nine to eleven inches in height, and those over eleven inches. In this case, "q" is used for the second size, and "f" ("folio") for the largest. But this adds to the confusion of the public and should be done only for the most pressing of reasons.

Reference books must also be identified by "R" or "Ref" or some such symbol above the class number on the spine of the books and, if the books are cataloged, on the catalog cards. The cards may also be stamped in the left margin to indicate location, e.g., "Reference book. Inquire at desk."

Other symbols are also used. Most public libraries have special collections for young adults; these may be marked "Y" on the spine. Public libraries also mark spines to indicate mysteries, westerns, collections of short stories, etc. These are not necessarily separated from other fiction; and if they are not, the mark on the spine (a colored disc or "spot") is all that is needed. Special collections such as those on local history, if separately housed, must be marked by a symbol. Books in foreign languages may be kept separate; in this case letters ("G" for German, "F" for French, "R" for Russian, etc.) designate language, as well as location. Designations of audio-visual and other nonbook materials are discussed in Chapter 14.

Use of symbols requires careful planning. A list of all those used must be compiled and made available to the public. The same symbol cannot have two meanings: thus "R" cannot stand for Reference, Russian, and Records; nor "S" mean short stories, Spanish, and Slides.

To complicate the picture further, elementary school libraries frequently grade their materials for appropriate age level or school grade. The grade numbers may appear only at the upper right-hand corner of the shelf-list card.

The following rule of thumb may be helpful: If the symbol designates a separate shelving or housing for all copies of the work, it must appear on the catalog and shelf-list cards as well as on the materials themselves. If the symbol is used for separate shelving of only some copies (as perhaps for "Y"), it must appear on the material and on the shelf-list card but need not show on catalog cards. If the symbol does not disturb the shelf arrangement of the material, it appears only on the material itself and a notation is made on the shelf-list card to insure that all copies are marked uniformly.

Reader-Interest Classification

Some libraries have experimented with reader-interest classification, that is, large groupings of material around general interest topics such as "The Home," "Hobbies," "The Job," etc.

There are several ways to manage the details of establishing such groupings. One is to use the group term in place of the classification on the book and on all catalog cards; this commits one to leaving books in this arrangement permanently or to reclassifying them later if the arrangement should be changed. Another method is to classify regularly, then add to the catalog cards the group name by means of a stamp or penciled notation; this also means removing the marks if books are removed from their groups.

The books must also be flagged or marked in some way to insure their being returned to the desired shelves. This can be done by using colored dots on the spine—nail polish does this effectively—or by using special book cards; the latter slows up shelving, of course, since it requires the shelver to open every book.

Most libraries find that following a standard subject classification works best for the bulk of the collection, and they cater to special interests (which change from year to year) by means of exhibits or temporary groupings. Reference work and searches for individual titles are easier when each book has a definite location.

Copy Identification 9

Every copy of every publication which is circulated or loaned for use must have its own distinguishing designation to keep the holdings and circulation records accurate. Copy identification is not a necessity for materials which do not circulate since they are seldom duplicated. For these materials, the author, title, call number, and volume number (if applicable) distinguish each item.

Copy Numbers

It is possible to omit copy identification for the first copy of any book or other material. However, this can cause problems later if duplicate copies are added, so it is recommended that all copies be identified. The simplest method of copy identification in a single collection is to use copy numbers—the first copy of a title is copy 1, the second becomes copy 2, and so on. A record must be maintained of the number of copies of every title held by the library. The shelf list (see Chapter 10) keeps the record of cataloged books. However, if the library is or is likely to become part of a system of libraries or if the cataloging is done centrally for several libraries, the shelf-list record for all of the agencies may not be handy to the cataloging office. Even if it is, the assignment of copy numbers becomes involved and adds another step to the work. Copy numbering, furthermore, must be done as part of cataloging, whereas the step known as accessioning can be performed wherever it fits best in the procedures.

Accession Numbers

For the reasons cited above, the employment of a "copy identification" (or "accession") number is recommended. In this procedure, every book or piece to be cataloged is given a sequential number; the number is stamped or written in the book and is used in shelf-list and circulation records. The number may be a continuing sequence: the first book ever acquired is number 1, the next 2, and so on, forever. The disadvantage of this is that unbroken numbers are more difficult to type and to check accurately than those with some kind of break.

Such a break can be made by incorporating the year into the number. Thus the first book acquired in 1973 is given the number 73-1, the second 73-2, etc. If possible, an automatic stamping machine should be acquired. Larger libraries or processing centers handling many volumes use a seven- or eight-digit numbering machine—whichever length seems appropriate to the library's or system's annual acquisitions. In this case the first number is 73-0001 or 73-00001. The machine works by tens from the right-hand side, the tenth number in each row tripping the change in the next row; thus the number of digits is always the same. The same practice can be used for smaller numbers; 73-001, etc. Incorporating the date also gives additional information: it shows how many books were added in a given year and also the approximate age of each book. By recording in a small notebook the last number used each day—or week—or month—statistics and age can be more closely pinpointed. It is possible, of course, to combine numerals and letters in an accession number, but the last two advantages are then lost.

If stamping is done, the number is stamped on the book card and pocket and in the book, preferably on the first right-hand page following the title page. It is unsightly on the title page, and it should not be on the reverse of the title page because the stamping breaks the binding if pressure falls on the back of the book rather than on the bulked pages. Sometimes it is also possible to stamp the number directly onto the shelf-list card. Machines rarely have more than triple automatic repeats, but if a book card is not used or if the pocket is not stamped, one stamping is saved. A large operation, such as a processing center, may use a second machine for shelf-list stamping. It is also possible to buy a machine which repeats until hand-triggered to change to the next number; this requires strict attention on the part of the acessioner, for several books could be stamped with the same number should the accessioner neglect to trigger the number change.

The numbering is done where it best fits in the procedural chain. For an individual library or one with a central shelf-list record, it is perhaps best done before the cataloging starts so that the record on the shelf list can be typed as the rest of the typing is done. If the work is being done for a system of many libraries and the shelf-list cards are stamped, the stamping can come last in the process. Or the stamping (or copy assignment) can be done by the individual library after receiving the book from the center.

The Accession Book

The term *accession number* is an inheritance from the old accession book and continues to be used by librarians even though *copy identification* is more accurate, if more unwieldy. Not too many years ago every library maintained a large book in which were recorded (by hand, alas), for every book received, the author, title, publisher, source, date of acquisition, and the amount paid. The accession book still exists in some libraries, but the only reasons for it would seem to be (a) to serve as a substitute for the catalog in a very small collection, or (b) to meet some legal or regulatory requirement. If the latter is the case, it would be well to work to remove the regulation.

Use of Copy or Accession Numbers

In any discussion of copy numbers and accession numbers, the important point is that although the system may change (from accession number to copy number or from copy number to accession number), only one system of identification should be used at one time. It is nothing but waste motion to use both an accession number and a copy number on the same book. Volumes of a numbered set, of course, carry both the volume number and the accession (or copy) number, since it is entirely possible to acquire two or more copies of any volume.

Accession or copy numbers are never re-used, e.g., for a book replacing one lost or discarded. Re-use of numbers would throw the statistics off and also mislead as to the age of the new copy. Besides, one cannot be confident that a withdrawn book will never reappear.

Accession or copy numbers, to repeat, are stamped or typed or written in the book, on the book card and pocket, and on the shelf-list card. They are not shown on catalog cards and are not lettered on the spine of the book, since they are of no interest to the patron. They are not even needed for shelving, for it makes no difference which copy comes first if there are two or more.

10 The Shelf List

The shelf list is a file of cards—one entry for each title in the cataloged collection—arranged in the same order as the books on the shelf, that is, according to classification. On the shelf-list card, in addition to the call number and cataloging information, is a notation of every copy and every volume of the title held by the library.

Value and Use of the Shelf List

The shelf list becomes the inventory record and, as such, is possibly the most valuable record in the library. It is the basis for establishing the value of the collection, and sometimes is even insured itself. In case of fire or other catastrophe, it provides the basis both for rebuilding the collection and for damage claims. The shelf list is also one of the most useful records for the librarian's work. In book selection it is necessary to know the amount of material in a given subject area as well as how many copies there are of each title. In order work the shelf list is a handy source of information on bibliographical details and prices.

The classifier works constantly with the shelf list to see how books in certain subjects have been classed, to see how different class numbers have been applied, and also to determine when certain classes are getting too full and hence need to be subdivided. If the collection uses full call numbers (that is, uses Cutter numbers—see Chapter 8), the classifier also must check the number considered for a new book to make sure that it has not been used for another. And, of course, the shelf list is used in assigning copy numbers if they are used (see Chapter 9). In preparing bibliographies the shelf list is sometimes helpful. And it is used for statistical counts and records and as the tool in taking inventory. A very small library might get along without a catalog, but it would have difficulty in functioning without a shelf-list record.

Arrangement and Location of the Shelf List

The nonfiction entries in the shelf list are arranged according to classification number and then, within the same number, alphabetically by author. The numbers follow numerically up to the decimal point, then in decimal arrangement after the point. Thus, 620 precedes 621, but 621.24 precedes 621.3, and 621.99 precedes 622. Cards for fiction are kept separate (unless classified in 813, 823, etc.), arranged alphabetically by author and then, under author, by title. Individual biography may be inserted between 919 and 920 or kept separate, arranged first by the subjects' names, then by author, and then by title of the book. It is helpful to type the shelf-list card with the name of the biographee at the top of the card above the author's name; this makes it easier to use and file the biography section of the list. However, if a unit card containing tracing on the face of the card is used, the biographee's name can be underlined in the tracing. Other nonclassed books (picture books, etc.) are kept in separate files, alphabetically by author, then by title. Separate shelf-list files are kept for nonbook materials such as recordings, slides, etc. (see Chapter 14).

If books are Cuttered and a full call number is used, the shelf-list arrangement is exact: first by class number, then by author's letter, then by author's number, next by title, then by edition. The earliest edition comes first, the others following in chronological order. If the call number includes a date, the arrangement is also chronological.

The shelf-list cards are kept in easy-to-use file drawers of the same quality as those for the catalog, and, for easy consultation, the drawers should never be more than two-thirds full. The shelf list is kept handy to the area where the cataloging is done. It also helps to have it as accessible as possible to the reference and circulation work but never where it can be used by the public without close supervision. (Its records are too important to risk being marked, ink-spattered, rearranged, or otherwise tampered with.) And *no one* except the cataloger or his assistant is ever authorized to remove a card or change a card or record in the shelf list.

Information on the Shelf-List Card

The actual information included on a shelf-list card varies from library to library and from one era to another. Formerly it was considered time-saving to prepare the card with the briefest possible cataloging information. Recently, however, libraries have had occasion to regret this, and opinion now favors using a full catalog card giving all of the information included on the main entry card—in other words, using a unit card. Having this full information aids in classification and cataloging, often saving an extra checking in the catalog. Tracings, in particular, are needed. If printed cards are purchased or cards are machine-produced, it is actually quicker to acquire an extra card than to type a short-form shelf-list card; but even if the cards are typed, the extra minutes required to type a full card are saved over and over. An "S" penciled over the hole in the card or a stamped "Shelf list" identifies the shelf-list card so that it will not get into the catalog by mistake.

All copies and all volumes of a title are shown on the shelf-list card. If there is room on the face of the card, the holdings record is added there; if there is no room, or if the space runs out, the card is flipped and the record goes on the back. If needed, additional cards may be prepared and tied to the first.

Examples of holding records for a public library:

60-3	3.00	Accession numbers indicating copies and prices at
62-76	3.25	time of acquisition
63-60	3.25	
cop 1	3.00	Copy numbers used instead of accession numbers.
cop 2	3.25	

1959	59-7	3.00	Annual or added volumes or editions identified by
1960	60-10	3.25	date. Note 2 copies of 1960 volume, the second a
1960	60-175	g	gift.
1962	62-20	3.25	

v 1	58-7	6.50 v 1-3	Set with volume numbers. Note 2 copies of v.2, the
~~v 2~~	~~58-8~~		first having been withdrawn (lost or worn out).
v 3	58-9		Also note 6.50 is inclusive price of 3v. set.
v 2	61-15		

The price has to be noted on shelf-list cards, at least in a public library, in order to establish quickly the amount to be charged for lost books. It is also an aid in estimating the value of the collection for insurance purposes. And since in preparing a replacement order the shelf list must be checked to determine holdings in the library, jotting down the price at the same time saves looking it up in trade sources and helps to indicate the desired edition.

The price indicated is that charged the borrower who loses the book. If the actual (i.e., discount) cost is charged (as it is in some schools), the price given is that of actual cost; if the price charged is the list (retail) price, that is the one shown. A public library may charge its adult borrower the list price and the child a set price; in that case, the list price is used throughout; it is consistent and also is more helpful as ordering information. It is possible in a public library to charge more than the list price to pay for the costs of replacement. In such a case, it is sometimes advisable to code the price, raising it, say, to the next even dollar and giving it a symbol. Thus, books priced at $2.01 to $3.00 could be P3; $3.01 to $4.00, P4, etc. This coded price can then be included on the book card, and thus when a book is lost, the information is immediately available to the assistant responsible for overdues.

A school or church library will omit the price if borrowers are not charged for lost books.

If it is necessary to identify variations among individual copies, this information can be included in the accession record thus:

59-621	2.00	(Heath)	or	59-621	2.00	(Heath ed.)
60-15	2.25	(Doubleday)		60-15	2.25	(Doubleday,
60-78	2.25	"				Peters illus.)
62-153	3.50	(Follett)		60-78	2.25	"
				62-153	3.50	(Follett, preb.)

Or the name of the publisher of the first copy received may be included in the imprint on the shelf-list card only, in which case only variations from the first copy are noted in the accession information.

Inclusive listing on the shelf-list card, such as "copy 1-3," or "v.1-4" is never used, for if one copy or volume is withdrawn, complicated notation then becomes necessary to indicate what has been withdrawn and what remains. Taking inventory is also made more difficult if there is inclusive listing. Ditto marks can be used as indicated.

Formerly it was the practice to include in the accession information the date and source of acquisition. This does not serve any apparent need. If reordering, the library places the order with its current dealer regardless of the source of the copies previously acquired. There is some argument for including the date of acquisition if the copy-numbering system is used, but an accession number which includes the date shows the book's age closely enough.

11 Catalog Cards and Catalog Maintenance

Preparation of Cards

Catalog cards are made by individual libraries or library processing centers, using typewriters or other machines, or they are purchased ready-made. (See Chapter 12 for a discussion of card services.) Even if prepared cards are acquired, there is still some work to be done on them by the individual library. It is therefore necessary to have available a typewriter with a card platen, preferably one with an immovable steel strip inserted the length of the platen rather than a smaller clamp which rises and closes on a spring. The latter gets out of order frequently, wears out the platen more quickly, and does not permit rolling the platen backwards.

Typing directions for making cards are given in Appendix I. It is well to keep in mind that the more hand typing employed, the simpler should be the cards, for it takes time not only to type, but to proofread, and all typing must be revised letter by letter. Some information which can be accepted and used when found on a printed card can be omitted in typing. (See Chapter 6.)

Many copying machines have been tried by libraries in making their own catalog cards, but none are really successful in small operations. It has not proved to be efficient or economical to use machines for fewer than five copies per card; and since single, small libraries rarely need more than this, they are left with but three choices: to type all of their cards, to join a processing center or other cooperative group, or to purchase printed cards—or to combine two or all three of these methods. Some libraries have occasional access to a duplicating machine outside the library or have one machine for all library work; but use of such equipment means fitting the card work into other schedules, sometimes entails transporting material from one work area to another, and generally produces unacceptable work since different adjustments are required for cards and for paper work.

Catalog cards should be of good stock, exactly (preferably rotary) cut, and exactly punched with the hole in lower center. The so-called 3 x 5 card (which is actually $7\frac{1}{2}$ x $12\frac{1}{2}$ centimeters) is standard everywhere now, and no good can come of varying the size. Librarians no longer insist on a 100 per cent rag card, for it is more expensive, thicker, less flexible, and more difficult to use in a typewriter or copying machine than part-rag. It also soils just as quickly and, in time, tends to fuzz at the top. (Some soiling can be avoided by painting the tops of the cards with red ink. This is done by pushing all of the cards, purchased unbanded, tightly together in a box and applying the ink with a brush; it takes only a moment and is considerably cheaper than buying cards already edged.) Some of the library supply houses now sell a card which has no rag content but is acid free; this is cheaper even than part-rag, stands up well in tests, and, so far, in use. It is best to use unlined, plain white cards of medium weight.

Catalog Maintenance

A school library may need to maintain just one catalog and one shelf list; a public library needs at least two catalogs and two shelf lists, one each for adult and children's materials. The children have their own catalog for several reasons. If they have their own, on their eye level, they use it more easily, take a proprietary interest in it, and learn from it. Sometimes they experiment (rearranging or removing cards or guide cards) and this is easier to correct in the smaller catalog. They are not always deferential to adults if sharing the same one, and besides the children's and the adult collections are usually in separate areas. Most important, simpler entries and subjects are sometimes used for children, thus making interfiling with the adult cards difficult. There are other, more subtle, differences between cataloging for children and for adults. For instance, "Juvenile literature" is a legitimate subheading for a subject assigned to a book, but it is not one used in children's catalogs—it is redundant since all of the material in the juvenile collection is for children, and the child will *not* be drawn to any book so described.

The catalog case should be expertly made by experienced library suppliers to meet the following requirements: the drawers move easily and are neither too long nor too short; the rod holding the cards is true and strong; the cards move easily in the drawer; smoothly-sliding shelves are provided at the proper place; and the hardware (windows for labels, rod locks, and handles) is attractive, strong, easy to use, and rustproof. All of the drawers should be near eye level and easily reached. It is better to have fewer drawers per vertical row and to spread them farther in width, both for ease of use and to enable more people to use the catalog at the same time.

Drawers should never be more than three-quarters full; this allows enough space for cards to be pushed back and forth and remain fully exposed without having to be held. Proper allowance should be made for growth, so new cases will start with only a few inches of cards per drawer. The adjustable back block is moved to keep cards upright. When a case is outgrown, new sections are acquired (another reason for using standard makes which provide for expansion), and the cards are redistributed. This is done by pushing all cards of each drawer to the front and, holding them tightly together and upright, measuring them with a ruler. The total measurement in inches of all cards is divided by the number of drawers now available to give the number of inches of cards to be allotted to each. A blank card should be placed at the front and back of each drawer to absorb dust and dirt. The number of cards assigned to each drawer cannot be exactly the same, because the break between drawers should come at a convenient place in the alphabet: between "Def" and "Deg," for instance, rather than between "Defen" and "Defeo." In large catalogs, however, with hundreds of cards under a subject, such ideal breaks are seldom possible.

The labels for each drawer will show the contents of that drawer, and the whole alphabet must be covered though there may not be entries for every combination of letters shown. Thus, one drawer label would not end with "Debt" and the next start with "Deep" even though these are the key words on the cards at the break; the labels would in this case end with "Ded" and start with "Dee."

Strong and attractive guide cards should be interspersed among the cards approximately 1 to 1½ inches apart—less to start with since they get farther apart as the number of cards increases. If funds permit, it is possible to buy guides with tilted window-slot tabs; the transparent, angled tabs accommodate strips with printed or typed headings. Another attractive guide card is made of Mylar; it takes far less space than one made of cardboard and is reported to be as durable.

The word appearing on the guide should, for the most part, be a simple, short one which is likely to be used for a long time. For instance, one selects "Farm" rather than "Farm Animals," "Johnson" rather than "Johnson, Robert M.," or "Johanesen." (There will probably always be a Johnson in the catalog, but not always a Johanesen or a Robert M. Johnson.) It is simplest to use half-cut guides and alternate right- and left-hand ones.

For spots where the filing is complicated and difficult to understand, guides may be used to show the arrangement. Thus:

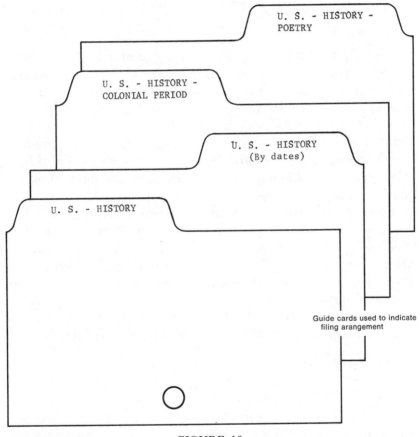

FIGURE 16

"How-to-use" cards should also be scattered through the catalog, one or two to a drawer. And directions for use of the catalog should be posted nearby. They should be in large print and should have diagramed card information, demonstrating author, title, subject. Such aids are available from library supply houses.

The catalog should be kept clean, attractive, and up to date. If cards or labels become soiled, they should be replaced. Clear plastic material can be cut and inserted in the drawer windows over the labels. Colored labels to match the decor of the room are effective and attractive, and they can be a help in keeping drawers in order since one color can be used for all drawers in a horizontal row. It is possible to obtain plastic covers to use over cards in sections getting very heavy use; these are also available with colored top borders, as are catalog cards with different-colored top edges for special use, e.g., for audio-visual materials, reference books, etc. (See Chapter 14.)

Filing

Although we say that in a dictionary catalog cards are alphabetically arranged, there are complications which require decisions. For instance, how do we file words or names of different spelling (basketball, basket ball; Smith and Smyth; catalog, catalogue)? How do we file prefixes (de, Mc, Mac, von)? What of surnames and forenames, abbreviations, numerals? The American Library Association has published a revised compilation of filing rules and an abridgment of the rules. The abridgment is adequate for a small catalog.

Some simple rules and examples are given in Appendix II of this manual; these recommend cataloging practices and filing which keep the arrangement simple and nearly alphabetical. After filing rules have been selected (those in the Appendix or those in the ALA compilation), they should be checked to indicate the library's choices and usage.

It is well to use not only guide cards to help indicate arrangement but also many explanation cards or references, such as:

> Base ball
> *see*
> Baseball

The more cards there are filed at one time, the less time need be taken per card; therefore it is efficient to keep new cards arranged in a separate file (at the end or beginning of the catalog), interfiling when several hundred have accumulated. However, some libraries prefer more frequent filing, sacrificing some efficiency for the sake of improved service. The cards can and should be arranged and filed in the preliminary file by clerks, pages, volunteers, or student assistants. When the time comes to file into the main part of the catalog, the clerk or student does the preliminary filing, either leaving the cards above the rods or inserting a "filing" card before each card filed. This filing card should be heavy, of a bright color, cut one quarter of an inch taller than the catalog cards, and with a keyhole notch in the bottom center permitting it to be lifted out without removing the rod. The advantage of using such a device is that it is the filer, and not the cataloger, who takes the time to remove and replace the rods; it also means that the drawers can be put back into the case without cards being lost or damaged. Further, service is not interrupted, and the revising can be done when convenient. The filer keeps a list of the drawers in which new cards have been filed. The filing cards can be used over and over again since the reviser removes them as he corrects the filing. These filing cards are available from library supply houses.

Filing should be revised by the librarian responsible for the cataloging, for he is not only checking the proper arrangement but is also watching for errors in cataloging, noting where guides or references are needed, looking for "dead" or questionable cards, watching for subjects requiring subdivision, and so forth.

12 Cataloging Services

A librarian in the United States need not feel he is alone or has to pioneer; there is abundant help and advice all about him. First, there is much in print designed to inform him, and often there is an experienced librarian in the community or nearby who will be only too happy to help a newcomer or a beginner. Most important, a great many states have a state library or state library extension service to advise public libraries, and state or regional school library supervisors to help school libraries; this is the primary concern of these offices. Many churches foster church libraries, preparing guidance manuals and offering advice from their central offices. Information is supplied through the mail by library schools and large libraries, as well as by the Bureau of Libraries and Educational Technology of the United States Office of Education. Salesmen from library supply houses can be helpful; most of them sincerely want to assist each library to find the supplies and equipment that are best for its needs. Moreover, studying supply-house catalogs is an education in itself.

Published Cataloging Information

In addition to the essential cataloging tools cited in Chapter 1, there are many other publications which give help to the cataloger and classifier. No matter how small it is, the library will undoubtedly subscribe to *The Booklist*; this carries a selected list of new books in each issue, showing for each an annotation, the proper author and title, the Dewey Decimal classification, the Library of Congress card number (for ordering cards from LC), and suggested subjects. The H. W. Wilson Standard Catalog series, which includes *Senior High School Library Catalog, Junior High School Library Catalog, Children's Catalog, Fiction Catalog,* and *Public Library Catalog,* gives complete cataloging and classification information, and any library should have at least one of them. The suggestions made in all of these tools are appropriate for small libraries, including school libraries, and can be followed if they agree with the individual library's cataloging policies.

Library of Congress cataloging is now given in full in the weekly listing of new books in *Publishers Weekly*, and this information is cumulated in the monthly *American Book Publishing Record* (BPR), as well as in the LC catalogs of printed cards. The last mentioned will probably not be in the small library, but may be available in another local library. *Book Review Digest* and *Cumulative Book Index* also carry helpful information, matching that of LC. The LC cataloging is most helpful in indicating authors and in suggesting classification and subjects; however, the small library should not follow it blindly—the classification is often too detailed, the authors (particularly corporate authors) too complex, the subjects too specific or too technical. Publishers' catalogs usually provide information on the subject coverage of the books listed, and so, of course, do all reviewing magazines. The cataloger of the small library must learn to check all sources of information but must use them judiciously.

In July 1971 the Library of Congress, in cooperation with many American publishers, inaugurated its Cataloging in Publication Program. Using prepublication material supplied by participating publishers, LC provides the publishers with cataloging information prior to a book's publication so that the information can be printed in the book itself. At the close of the CIP Program's first year, over 200 publishers were participating, and 6,500 titles had been processed. As CIP develops, the immediate availability of cataloging information for most American trade publications should speed the availability of new books for library users, reduce cataloging costs, and thus release more of a library's funds for the purchase of additional books. This kind of program has long been needed, and it should benefit both libraries and publishers.

Another recent Library of Congress project for the dissemination of cataloging information is MARC (Machine-Readable Cataloging). Through this program cataloging information is supplied on tape in machine-readable form. This program will not benefit directly as many small libraries as the CIP Program, unless the libraries have computer time available to them in neighboring institutions.

Printed Cards

Printed (or processed) catalog cards are available from many sources. The Library of Congress, as it catalogs books for its collections, prints extra copies of the cards and sells them. This cataloging is for a very large library which includes materials from all over the world and in every language, so that the cataloging is appropriate only for the largest high schools and the adult collections of public libraries of some size. Some publishers now obtain printed catalog cards for their books and distribute a set in each copy; but there is no way to know this in advance. Some of these cards can be used as they are, some can be adapted, all will give some help to the cataloger.

The H. W. Wilson Company has been printing and selling cards since 1938, and these cards are designed specifically for the school and small public library. Entries are simple, descriptive cataloging is brief, appropriate subjects and classification are indicated, and annotations are included on the cards. They are available only in sets and with subject headings, added entries, and Dewey classification numbers printed at the top. A set of cards includes one author or main entry card, one card for each added and subject entry indicated, and one author card for shelf-list use.

Some libraries order cards when ordering a book even though it results in some wasted cards if the book is not received. Ordering cards also takes time on the library's part: the catalogs or lists must be searched to locate card numbers or to see if cards are available; orders must be prepared; and the cards, when received, must be checked against the order and brought together with the books. Records must be maintained for unfilled orders. Then in some cases adjustments must be made in accordance with local policy, and cards changed or retyped. If all of this holds up cataloging the books and interferes with service, particularly for adult books in a public library, the books should be classified with the help of printed information and released, after a brief penciled record has been made for a temporary file. If needed, temporary cards can even be made for the catalog and shelf list; such cards should be flagged, or colored cards should be used, so that they will not be overlooked indefinitely. Occasionally, a change in author may require rehandling a book so prepared—correcting the entry on book card and pocket, relettering the spine, and so forth—but such occasional rehandling is not so serious as holding the book out of circulation. The lists of Wilson cards available now include the classification number for each title. The books can therefore be classified correctly even though the cards have not yet come.

The time and cost of purchasing cards must be weighed against the greater cost of doing all of the work in the library. Nor is cost the only consideration; the caliber of the work and the appearance of the cards are also important.

Centralized or Cooperative Services

Cards are sometimes available from sources closer to the library. Springing up all over the country are centralized processing centers for cataloging and making cards, as well as various other services such as buying, lettering, and jacketing. These are varied in organization—single counties, groups of counties, states, regions, sections. Some are cooperative, with all libraries in a group combining their resources; some are organized so that one library supplies the service to others on a contract basis; some are part of a central unit such as a state or country library or a school system. These cooperative or centralized ventures do not necessarily save a great deal of money; but being able to afford specialists, better equipment, better tools, they provide more uniform and better work than the single library, and their services enable the individual librarians to devote more time to serving their patrons in reference, reader advisory guidance, book selection, and community work.

Commercial Services

There are also commercial firms which will handle any or all of the processing steps for a fee. Some studies have shown these services to be more expensive than centralized or cooperative processing organizations, but the latter are not always available, and, in each case, it is worth while to see what the services have to offer. Even if not used all of the time, they certainly can help in such emergencies as critical staff shortages, opening a new library or enlarging or reorganizing one, or periods of rush spending. They will do as much or as little as the library asks, but there are always some things that only the individual library itself can do: checking names and subjects against its own usage, making necessary cross references, accessioning or assigning copy numbers, adding accession information to its shelf list, and filing the cards.

Commercial cataloging and processing services have multiplied to such an extent in recent years that the Resources and Technical Services Division of the American Library Association sponsored the publication of a directory of such services. This directory, compiled by Barbara M. Westby, appeared in *Library Resources and Technical Services*, Spring 1969, vol. 13, no. 2, pp. 220-286.

Physical Preparation of Materials 13

Books and other library materials must be physically prepared for the shelves and for circulation. They require marks of ownership, circulation devices (book cards, if used, and pockets to carry them, and date-due slips), lettering and other spine markings, jacketing, and, for unbound materials, special strengthening. These procedures, like all others, must be fitted into the work where they can be done most efficiently and most expeditiously. It is work which can and should be done by the lowest-salaried assistants—student assistants (volunteer or paid), pages, or clerks. With careful planning it can be done quickly but exactly; bad or careless work can result in defacing the material, spoiling its attractiveness, or actually reducing its usefulness. New products which lead to new and improved ways of doing the work become available every day, so the methods need continuous study and improvement.

Information in the Book

Today it is not considered necessary to record full acquisition or accession information in the book. In public libraries the price (whichever price is recorded on the shelf list) may be noted on the slip or order card left in the book for shelf-listing or penciled lightly in the book itself. The first right-hand page following the title page is a good place for all information—call number, price if needed, copy or accession number, and, if work is done for more than one agency, the symbol of the agency. Some libraries use the back of the title page, but leaning on it to write or stamp on it breaks or weakens the back of the book, and the indentations show through and mar the title page. If it is known from the order that the book is a duplicate, it saves work to have this indicated on the order card accompanying the book or by penciling in "dup" in the book where the call number is placed or by some other device such as underlining the price. When checking books against bills, new titles should be separated from added copies or added volumes to expedite the cataloging work.

Ownership Marks

Some stamping is necessary to identify ownership in order to aid in the return of a straying book and to discourage theft, but perforations should *never* be used. The stamping also serves as advertising; people on the street seeing others carrying interesting-looking books with the name of the library showing may become inspired to seek the service. Books need not be stamped inside. It is best to stamp just once or possibly twice—across the top or bottom while the book is held closed. The marking is both visible and difficult to remove, and it can be done quickly by tipping a stack of books toward one's body and, holding them firmly with one hand and arm, stamping down the pile. They can then be turned over on the other side and stamped. Stamps in two sizes will take care of most books: one stamp about three quarters of an inch in height, one about three eighths of an inch. It is well to do the stamping just after the books have cleared the ordering procedures in order to establish ownership. If book pockets are used, they may be stamped (or they may be acquired preprinted with the name of the library).

The rest of the preparations work will come after cataloging and after the call number has been penciled in the book and the book card and pocket have been prepared. The book card and pocket carry the accession number or copy number, price if desired, call number or class designation, author's surname, and short title. The book pocket is pasted in; simple and inexpensive pasting machines are available if there is work enough to justify filling and cleaning them. Strangely, there can be considerable disagreement over where the pocket goes—front or back of the book, on inside cover or on flyleaf; actually it can't make very much difference—the library should use whichever location is best for its circulation procedures. The location should be the same in all books to speed the procedures. If plastic jackets are applied, the pocket must go on the flyleaf since the jacket overlaps the inside front and back covers. Date-due slips, if used, are also pasted on the flyleaf at this time; printed and gummed slips are available from library supply houses, as, of course, are pockets and book cards.

Lettering on Spine

The next step is the lettering or marking. There is considerable study going on now to find better ways of lettering book spines, but most of the new ways are for large operations, involving specially equipped typewriters, irons for burning in call numbers, etc. The small library is still better off lettering by hand with either black india ink or white engrossing or artist's ink (whichever shows up best on the particular book). A pen or fine brush is used, and letters and numbers are made as square and unslanted as possible. Most students can soon learn to do this. If the library can afford it, a small electric stylus which transfers pigment from paper onto the spine produces marking which will not chip off. And the library supply houses have papers with numbers and letters printed in transfer ink—by moving the paper about over the spine and rubbing appropriately marked areas with a pencil, quite professional-looking call numbers can be made; it is expensive and slow, but not too much so for the small operation. If white ink is hand-applied, a swipe of clear shellac over the number makes it last longer. It is difficult to get anything to stick to waterproof materials used on some books; occasionally, however, ammonia or alcohol will remove the gloss and make the material more receptive to lettering.

If plastic jackets are used, pressure labels are applied, those with "permanent" glue being preferred. Such labels are on sheets and can be lettered with pen and india ink or typewriter, then removed from the backing paper and pasted on book jackets or paperbound books. A book to be jacketed is *not* also lettered on the spine of the book itself; by the time the jacket is gone, most books are ready for rebinding or discarding, and it is easier to mark the few needing it than to mark all, often unnecessarily. Call numbers should, so far as possible, appear in the same location on all books so that the books look tidy on the shelves and can be more easily shelved and located. A piece of cardboard can be used as a measure. If the book is too narrow to carry the number horizontally, it can be turned and lettered vertically; when this is done, the marking should always run in the same direction, preferably top to bottom, to make shelving and checking of shelves easier.

If special marking is needed to restrict circulation, as for reference books, or to locate special or separately shelved collections, such as short stories, westerns, mysteries, and books for young adults, symbols may be made part of the call number ("R" or "Ref"), or printed discs ("spots") may be pasted on the spine. If author or biographee or other designation is needed for shelving, the name or word is underlined with ink, or, if not there, lettered on the spine.

Plastic Jackets

Transparent jackets (called plastic but made of acetate or Mylar) applied to books over colorful dust jackets have done much to dress up libraries and "sell" books, particularly in public libraries. Whenever used, they are extremely popular, and they also save binding expenditures since, with ordinary care, a jacket will give a book twice as many circulations as it would have without it. Each of the library supply houses has its own style of jacket, and the library should choose the one which seems most appropriate and easiest to acquire, stock, and apply. Some have paper backing which makes them wear longer and makes them easier to apply; but it also means carrying more stock since they come in one-eighth-inch size variations and must be fitted exactly. Without the backing, one jacket can be adjusted to fit several sizes. Jackets may be applied with tape, but pasting the overlap directly to the inside covers of the book is advised (particularly for children's books) to prevent removal. Mylar jackets are the strongest and the most expensive; they do not shrink or expand in temperature change and do not tear, although they can be cut, punched, gouged, or burned.

Some libraries use the jackets for all books; others exclude reference or other noncirculating books, prebound picture books, or other categories. Some libraries use them only for popular or special reading collections, but in general their use is increasing.

The final step in the preparations is revising (inspecting) the work, that is, making sure that everything needed is taken care of and that the call numbers, names, and titles match in all places where used. The revising and shellacking can be done at the same time, thus saving one handling.

Special Materials and Treatment

Materials other than books often require special treatment, as, indeed, may some books. If pages are uncut, they should be carefully cut with a bone cutter; loose plates or plates loosely attached should be glued down. Each plate in a portfolio needs to be stamped with ownership and lettered in pencil with the call number. Supplements laid in a book, such as folded maps or illustrative material, answer books, etc., should have a pocket provided to hold them or else be removed, marked with call number or author, and separately shelved, possibly in a vertical file; the book from which such material has been taken must be marked to indicate where the missing material is located.

Audio-visual and other nonbook materials all require special preparation; see Chapter 14 for details.

Some of the work can be done in the library, some requires a commercial binder's assistance. Products available to help with much of it include such items as pamphlet boxes, pamphlet binders, plastic sleeves or special holders for recordings, etc. The binders and the library supply houses have worked on many of the problems and can give advice.

Mending

Nothing detracts from a library's appeal more than a shabby book collection. Dirty, ragged, and smelly books repel the most ardent reader; and keeping books clean, bright, and mended is a continuing and important responsibility.

Some books, especially those bound specifically for library use, are covered with washable cloth. Shellacking or spraying the backs helps oftentimes to bring back the color, and art gum can be used to remove pencil markings.

As books are checked in from circulation, as they are shelved or used, or as those on the shelves are checked, the librarian or assistant should always look at them critically to spot torn pages, splitting backs, loose cases, and other signs of wear and tear, and to see if the plastic jackets are torn. Quick mending can be done in the library—mending a page or two (using transparent, flexible, paper mending tape), running paste between the spine and book cover at the joints, or tightening the book into the cover with a strip of double-stitched binding obtained from a library supply house.

Unless free student or other help is available, mending beyond this point usually doesn't pay; the book should be replaced or it should be rebound. A little study will determine how much mending each library can afford. Most of the supply houses have mending materials and publish booklets of mending directions. They will also arrange mending demonstrations at library meetings. But amateurish mending with "make-do" or inappropriate materials should be avoided like the plague.

14 Audio-Visual and Other Nonbook Materials

The Importance of Nonbook Materials

The information explosion of recent decades has involved a tremendous increase not only in the publishing of books but also in the production of nonbook materials: motion pictures, filmstrips, slides, microforms, recordings, maps, periodicals, newspapers, pamphlets—and the list continues to grow. A library cannot be effective today if it does not make some of these materials available to its users.

All must be organized for use, and, because of their variations in physical form and other complexities, a great deal of time and consideration is required merely to make decisions concerning their handling. In fact, the whole area has been moving so rapidly that most librarians find themselves making rules daily to fit the new problems, and practices have not had time to settle into accepted, uniform, and recorded patterns. It may not take more time actually to handle these materials, but it takes a disproportionate amount of time to discuss them and decide how to handle them.

The forms of nonbook materials generally preclude their being shelved along with books. Some types require metal cases, some need specially constructed shelves, and for others upright (or vertical) files are necessary.

Since processing and other kinds of organization of materials are dependent on use, and since in different types of libraries use varies more for these materials than for books, it may be well to consider some of the differences among the libraries.

In Different Kinds of Libraries

The public library is in direct contact with people of all ages, of all social, economic, cultural, and educational backgrounds. While it uses some of its materials in public programs, the greatest use is in direct loans of material either to be taken from the library or to be used in reference and individual research within the building or room. The library's materials (nonbook as well as book) must be made accessible to its patrons as quickly as possible. Segregation of the nonbook materials allows library users to browse in some of these collections just as they do at the bookshelves. However, there should also be an approach to these materials through a catalog—either the general catalog or a separate card file. Cards may be added to the catalog reminding the person gathering material on a subject (as for a program) of the availability of nonbook materials. These are usually information cards under subjects rather than catalog cards for individual items. Or, for certain categories (as records) the catalog cards may be kept near the materials themselves rather than in the general catalog.

The school library largely serves two more or less homogeneous groups: the students attending the school and the faculty teaching those students. While it conducts programs on its own, promotes reading, loans materials, and gives reference services, its nature is fundamentally educational, and its center is the curriculum. Consequently, the subject approach to materials is more important than their form, and school libraries gain by having cards for all materials in a single ("integrated") catalog. Regardless of the debate over whether the curriculum center or instructional materials center should be a part of the library or a partner to it, the fact remains that many school libraries do have charge of the special teaching materials and must organize them. Even when the curriculum center is separate from the library, most school librarians favor the library's having cards for the center's materials in the card catalog. Many school libraries also have responsibility for organizing and maintaining a professional library for the teaching staff of the school or school system. The materials are prepared, then, for three broad services: to provide conventional library service to the student directly, to furnish background professional reading for the teacher, and to provide the teaching materials for the teachers to use with the students in the classrooms.

The church or parish library is urged not to become just another lending library, but to serve as an adjunct to the church's activities. It provides specialized materials to lend for reading and also provides materials for teaching and other church and Sunday school activities. It may in addition have responsibility for the official histories and papers of the church. Its audo-visual materials will seldom be loaned but will be used in classes, programs, or church services and will be located by the librarian.

General Considerations

Certain matters need to be decided in regard to nonbook materials generally. First, where will they be kept? Will they be available to the public using them? Will they be assigned a subject number based on the classification scheme used by the library? Will they then be shelved, if physically possible, alongside the books in the same class? Or will they be kept in separate files or cases, special shelving, or special areas? If the last, does the subject classification really help, or is it easier and more efficient to use an accession number with the items in each category thus arranged by order of receipt? Will the materials be cataloged, that is, have catalog cards made for them? Will these cards be kept in separate files grouped by category, kept separate but interfiled with other nonbook materials, or filed in the general card catalog? Will those cards in the general catalog have a different color for each type of material? In schools, is the grade level indicated; if so, how? In children's collections, is age level indicated, and, if so, how?

The decisions depend on the type of the library, the proposed use of the materials, considerations of care and preservation, and the nature of each kind of material. In this area no particular practices can be recommended for all small libraries.

Many libraries use symbols (e.g., "FS for filmstrips, "M" for maps, etc.) which are made part of the designated number (subject classification or accession), as M940 (map of Europe), FS280 (Filmstrip number 280). Colors have been used by some to designate different categories, for example, blue for filmstrips, pink for records, etc. Plastic card covers with colored tops are also available. With the wider use of machine-made cards and the photocopying of cards for various uses, the time has come to consider dropping the use of colors. A stamp with the word "Map" or "Filmstrip," or other designation can be used at the upper left-hand corner of the appropriate cards. This indicates the category to every user. If accession numbers are used, a simple record must be kept to indicate the last number used. Provision must also be made for keeping statistics on additions and withdrawals. This can be done by means of a catalog card placed at the beginning of the shelf-list section devoted to the particular material. Thus a card before the listings of filmstrips would be lined off with spaces for additions and withdrawals for each year, totaled at the end of of the year.

Cataloging Rules

The rules for nonbook materials presented in the *Anglo-American Cataloging Rules* were designed primarily for the general research library, and they do not provide for all of the types of nonbook materials available at the present time. In 1973, the Canadian Library Association published *Nonbook Materials: The Organization of Integrated Collections*. The authors of this work consulted with the Advisory Committee on the Cataloging of Nonbook Materials, composed of representatives of the Canadian Library Association, American Library Association, Association for Educational Communications and Technology, and the Educational Media Association of Canada. The rules were developed according to the principles of the *Anglo-American Cataloging Rules* and their application makes possible an integrated catalog for books and nonbook materials.

The methods of treating nonbook materials recommended in this manual, which is intended for school and small public libraries, are based on the two sources mentioned in the preceding paragraph. The rules for cataloging and the means of organizing these materials have been simplified in accordance with the policy applied in the preceding chapters to other materials.

For those nonbook materials which are not cataloged but which are entered on catalog cards with a subject heading, it is most important that the subject heading be selected from the list of subject headings used for the fully cataloged material. Even though these cards may be filed in a separate file, the users should not be confused by a different group of subject headings. Furthermore, if it is decided later to interfile these cards in the general catalog, there will be no conflict of headings.

In the following pages, the treatment recommended for some types of nonbook materials provides for main entry under title. If a person or corporate body is responsible for the intellectual or artistic content of the work, an added entry under the person or body may be made if it is considered desirable; this optional procedure has not been included as a directive under some of the specific rules or recommendations.

The upper left corner of the catalog card should indicate the type of material described on the card—for example, Diorama, Globe, Kit, Study Print. The designation should be the same as that used after the title in the body of the card. If there are enough examples of one type of material to make it worth while, a small rubber stamp may be purchased; otherwise, the designation should be typed in the upper left corner. If the items are given accession numbers, the number appears below the stamp in the left margin, thus forming a call number for the specific item.

Motion Pictures and Motion Picture Loops

Motion pictures are entered under title, followed by subtitle and the designation "(Motion picture)." If a title frame is lacking, the title is taken from the leader, the container, or other sources; if the title is lacking or cannot be determined, an appropriate title is supplied by the cataloger. The sponsor is given following the designation "(Motion picture)," then the producer, after the phrase "Made by." If the releasing agent differs from the producer, that name is noted also.

The date of release is included after the name of the releasing company; if this date is not known, the copyright is given after the name of the producer. If neither date can be determined the probable date of release is given with a question mark—for example, 1970?

Collation includes: length in running time to nearest minute; indication of sound (sd.) or silent (si.); color (col.) or black and white (b & w); and width in millimeters (35mm).

If the film is part of a series, the series note is given in the usual position.

Other notes are included when necessary to amplify the physical description (particularly when special equipment is required), and to give credits and cast if desirable.

A summary, describing the content of the film objectively and succinctly, is the last item before the tracings.

Motion pictures may be arranged by accession number, following the designation "MP." The film, film case, and catalog cards carry this number. The number may be written on the film in white ink with a special pen or fine brush.

```
Motion
picture
MP10        We hold these truths. [Motion picture]   FILMCOM, 1966.
               25 min.  sd.  color.  16 mm.

               Magnetic sound track.
               CREDITS: Producer and director, Stephen G. Williams.
               SUMMARY: Explains some of the approaches used by The Institutes for the
            Achievement of Human Potential in Philadelphia, Pa., to help brain-injured
            children reach their potential.
                                                    Catalog card for a motion picture

               1. Institutes for the Achievement of Human Potential.   2. Mentally hand-
            icapped children—Philadelphia.   3. Mentally handicapped children—Educa-
            tion—Philadelphia.     I. Institutes for the Achievement of Human Potential.
            II. Filmcom.

            [HV899]              ◯      362.3                72-700611
                                                                 MARC
            FILMCOM
            for Library of Congress        72                         F
```

FIGURE 17

Motion picture loops are brief motion pictures, usually contained in cartridges. If loops are cataloged, the rules for motion
pictures are applied, with the following exceptions: (1) the designation "(Motion picture loop)" is added after the title; (2) the
"Made by" phrase may be omitted; (3) the date used is that on
the film loop or case; and (4) if the loop is in a cartridge, this fact
is noted in the collation.

Filmstrips

A filmstrip is a roll of film containing successive images, usually to be viewed at one time. Filmstrips are entered under title
unless they are reproductions or adaptations of printed material,
in which cases they are entered under the heading for the printed
form. The title is taken from the title frame rather than the
leader frame, which is separated from the main body of the filmstrip by a length of blank film.

If the frames are numbered, the total number of frames is included in the collation. For a filmstrip with unnumbered frames,
the collation indicates "1 roll."

Notes are added at the discretion of the cataloger. (See Appendix I, page 165.)

Slides

Slides are usually kept in slide trays and are viewed in a slide viewer or projector. They are generally entered under title, although art slides are entered under the name of the artist. The word "(Slide)" follows the title. The collation gives the number of slides and the size.

The rules for slides apply to stereoscope slides, except that "(Stereoscope slide)" is used after the title, and the collation includes the number of double frames—for example: 7 double frames.

```
Slide
S106        Brazil builds (Slide)   American Council on
               Education, 1945.
               32 slides   col.   2 x 2 in.
```

Catalog card for a slide

FIGURE 18

Transparencies

A transparency is an image produced on transparent material and is to be used with an overhead projector. Transparencies are entered under title, followed by the word "(Transparency)." If a title is not given, one is supplied by the cataloger.

The collation includes the number of pieces and the size of the transparency. A transparency with overlays is considered "1 piece." Notes are added to explain the collation, if necessary, and to indicate use.

Microforms

Microforms (microfilms, microcards, microprint, and microfiche) have not been widely adopted in small libraries, but public libraries large enough to keep files of newspapers and magazines are finding microfilms worth while even though they require the use of a reader. The film saves binding and shelving cost, and it solves the mutilation problem. Cheaper and better readers are becoming available, and films no longer have to be kept in special humidity-controlled cases.

Material in microform is cataloged according to the rules for the material of which it is a reproduction. The designation "(Microfilm)," "(Microfiche)," etc. is added after the title.

The collation includes the number of pieces—for example: 1 reel, 6 cards, 3 boxes of cards. For microfilm, the size is given in millimeters; for cards, the size of the mount is used. Notes are added if necessary.

Records for microforms of serials, periodicals, or newspapers are entered in the same shelf list for the bound volumes. A microform shelf list for books is best kept in a separate file, arranged by the number assigned to the microform; the number might be the call number of the book it reproduces with a microform designation or the microform designation with an accession number.

Phonodiscs and Phonotapes

Phonodisc is the term used for phonograph records, recordings, and audiodiscs. Phonodiscs are made in different speeds ($16\frac{2}{3}$, $33\frac{1}{3}$, 45, and 78 rpm, i.e., revolutions per minute); they are also available for either monophonic or stereophonic record players. The early 78's were thick and easily broken or damaged; for that reason and because of the fact that they are rapidly going out of print, they are no longer in use in libraries except for historical or "listening" collections. Newer 78's are occasionally bought to secure certain recordings of sound effects, children's material, or material not otherwise available. The 45's are, for the most part, recordings of popular music and hence not acquired for library use, except, again, for some children's records. The $33\frac{1}{3}$'s (the "long-playing" records or LP's) constitute the bulk of library collections. The very slow $16\frac{2}{3}$'s for very long playing (as for the bedridden or the blind) are becoming of more interest to public libraries.

Recordings are probably the most complex material to process; and possibly public and school libraries differ most in ways of handling them, since the public library's chief concern is lending them for home use and the schools use them primarily as teaching aids.

The first decisions are concerned with location and arrangement. Location influences arrangement; both decisions depend upon who will have access to the recordings and what will be the approach. And the decisions influence the cataloging details required. Decisions are based on such questions as the following: Will the music and nonmusic records be divided? Will records for children's use be separate from those for adults, or students' collections separate from teachers' materials? Will recordings be divided first by speed? Will the arrangements be by manufacturers' numbers, by accession numbers, alphabetical by composer or author, or by broad or exact subject groups? If the arrangement is by subject, will it follow Dewey, LC, or some special scheme? Libraries have employed dozens of combinations of arrangements, but the majority of those not tied to past decisions tend to choose one of three; (1) accession number, (2) author or composer, (3) subject.

For a small collection in a public library, accession number is the simplest. The number provides identification for circulation purposes, and, it is argued, since few recordings are available at a given time and those few kept in one display case, the patron can go through all of those displayed to make his choice. From the catalog he can choose and reserve a specific work. As the collection grows, it becomes more difficult for the patron to find what he wants among the records, and he must depend more on the catalog. If the collection is not accessible to the patron, he must make all of his selections from the catalog. For these reasons, the arrangement does not matter, and recordings are shelved most easily by accession number. Author and composer arrangement is not so easily handled in closed shelves and is little more helpful on the open shelves since patrons generally tend to select by form and since so many long-playing records have no author or else have several.

A subject arrangement is perhaps best for schools since it conforms with the placement of other materials and since the classification groups the musical records by form (opera, symphony, voice, etc.). A symbol may be employed, such as Rec782 or Disc 782. In some public libraries, children's collections are divided by age interest with color used as the code device.

Musical recordings are most often cataloged, from the label, by composer, with added entries for subject (i.e., musical form), performer, instrument, arranger, and, if distinctive, title. Separate cataloging is done for each work on a record or in an album. If the works are many or by many composers, or if there is no composer (as folk music), the main entry is under the title. Information on the card includes composer, arranger, soloist or performing group, manufacturer's name, record number, number of sides, size, speed, and title of recording on reverse side. If there are more than two works on a record, a contents note may be added. If the recording has accompanying material (libretto, contents, historical notes, etc.) it is best kept with the records, as in a pocket pasted in the back of the album or record holder. If this is not advisable, the material is marked with the call number of the record and filed in a vertical file. A note must then be made on the catalog cards, e.g., "Miniature score in pocket" or "Libretto in Vertical File." The book card must include all pieces, e.g., "6 records, miniature score," so that, when the work is returned from circulation, the person receiving it can check at once to make sure all is accounted for. Note of any damage or missing part should be made (in ink) on the book pocket so that later borrowers will not be held responsible.

Nonmusical records are cataloged under author. If there is no author or there are many, the title is used. Thus, John Barrymore's reading of Shakespeare is under Shakespeare; Edward R. Murrow's "I Can Hear It Now" is under title. Dame Edith Sitwell reading her own poetry is under her name, but if she read from several writers, the entry would be under title. Usually the cards, appropriately stamped, will be filed in the main catalog. Some public libraries, however, prefer a small separate catalog kept handy to the record collection. (See Appendix I, pages 165-167.)

Uniform titles are used as appropriate, just as for books (see pages 51-53) and for music. When a uniform title is used, it is followed by the term "(Phonodisc)"; otherwise, the term follows the actual title of the record.

Single records are placed in protective covers or containers obtained from library supply houses; albums may be pasted to these holders, or used as they are. Records have call number and name of library lettered on the seal, and on the sleeve, album, or holder. Book cards and pockets are prepared and inserted in album or holder or pasted to the sleeve.

Recordings are shelved in special shelves which permit each to stand upright, preferably each in its own compartment. "Tubs" or display racks, such as those used in music stores, may be used for a small collection kept in the reading room. Care must be taken, of course, to prevent damage. Records should be handled only by the edges and should not be stacked. They must be protected from spilled ink and shellac and kept away from heat.

A phonotape is a sound recording on magnetic tape. Phonotapes are cataloged according to the rules used for phonodiscs, with these exceptions: (1) the term "(Phonotape)" is used in place of "(Phonodiscs)," (2) collation indicates open reel-to-reel tape, cassette, or cartridge; speed for reels; and stereo, if the tape is stereophonic rather than monaural. Notes are added as necessary or desirable.

Pamphlets, Pictures, Clippings, Study Prints

The physical difference between a pamphlet and a paperbound book is technically only the difference in size, since pamphlets usually are defined as separate publications of less than fifty (or one hundred) pages. Librarians tend to separate them on the basis of content, thinking of the pamphlet as a special treatment of a specific subject.

Most pamphlets are short-lived but valuable because they give information more up to date than books; a few have real permanent value. There are four or more different ways of treating them: (1) If of sufficient value and anticipated long life, they may be cataloged, classified, accessioned, shelf-listed, supplied with book card and pocket, bound or put in pamphlet binder, and shelved—in fact, treated as a book. (2) Some pamphlets may be treated like paperbacks (see pages 121-122): stamped with ownership, given simple book cards and pockets, shelved in a separate collection, or shelved in their regular place on the shelves (without cataloging or shelf-listing). Some special materials which lend themselves to this treatment include paperbacked plays, holiday materials, house plans and decorator hints, paper books of recipes, librettos, Boy or Girl Scout booklets, rules for various sports, etc. (Such material is likely to be treated this way more by public libraries than by schools.) (3) Certain pamphlets of particular value to a subject may be given a general classification number preceded by a small "p," and dropped into a pamphlet box shelved at the beginning of the books in that classification. For instance, pamphlets on France might be lettered p914.4, contained in a box marked "France" and "p914.4," and shelved before the 914.4 books. Because of possible loss, this may not be wise for shelves open to the public, but it does save the librarian's time and makes the publications more easily accessible to the patron. (4) The most common way of treating pamphlets is to put them into folders or manila envelopes to be filed in a legal-size vertical file—the "Information File," "Pamphlet File," or "Vertical File." The pamphlet is stamped with ownership and with date of receipt and lettered on its face (upper left-hand corner) with a subject selected from the library's official list of subject headings. Each folder is devoted to a different broad subject, and a card list of the subjects used, plus a few cross-reference cards, is kept handy to the desk. Other libraries, school libraries particularly, put cards in the catalog under the subjects used, referring the user to the Vertical File. (See Appendix I, page 164.) Some libraries prepare book cards and pockets for pamphlets, but it is an expensive and time-consuming process. Others use slips or printed forms ("form cards") to charge them out, indicating number of pamphlets under each subject.

Subject:

Title:

Date:

No. of Pam.	No. of Pict.	No. of Mag.	Other

Above the line write subject if pamphlets or pictures, title and dates of issue if magazines. Use separate cards for separate subjects and separate magazine titles.

One library's form card used in circulating non-classified materials

FIGURE 19

Articles, pictures, news items, biographical sketches, charts, plans, etc., of local or curricular interest are often acquired or clipped for preservation. They must be dated and have their sources indicated on them. They are best mounted on sturdy cards, art paper, or mounting board (one to a sheet or two or three small ones on the same subject on one sheet); assigned broad subject headings; and put into the Pamphlet or Vertical File or in a separate file or files. If many pictures are kept or if larger ones are used, a special picture file may be established in steel cabinets for folders of pictures or special files permitting pictures and posters to be laid flat in sliding drawers. As with pamphlets, broad subjects are used and a card index is prepared. The cards may be kept in a separate index (in public libraries) or filed in the catalog (in school libraries). If kept in the catalog, cards should be stamped appropriately (for example, "Vertical File").

A study print is a picture (or pictures) with accompanying text which makes the picture more useful for study purposes. Study prints may be filed in the Pamphlet or Vertical File, or in a separate picture file if the library has one. On the catalog card the entry is under title, followed by "(Study Print)." The collation indicates the number of prints and the size of the mount. For a set containing a number of prints, it might be necessary to include a contents note if such a note would add any information not evident from the title.

Art Prints

Art prints may be added to the vertical or picture files, or they may be kept in a separate location. If the works are entered in a card file, the main entry is under the name of the artist. Following the title of the print are the words "(Art Print)." The cards should indicate whether the print is in black and white or color, and the size of the print.

Models, Dioramas, Realia

Models include globes, relief models, and other items.

A globe is a sphere with a map of the earth (terrestrial) or of the heavens (celestial). If a library has only one of each, it may not be necessary to provide any kind of entry for it. However, if it is considered desirable to record everything in the library's collection, globes may be cataloged according to the rules for maps (see pages 116-117), with the following exceptions: (1) the designation "(Globe)" or "(Celestial globe)" is used in place of "(Map)" after the title; (2) the diameter is given in the collation; and (3) the material of which the globe is constructed is mentioned in a note—for example: glass, plaster, etc.

A relief model is a three-dimensional map. Again, if the material is cataloged, the rules for maps are applied, except that (1) "(Relief model)" is used after title in place of "(Map)," and (2) the scale is noted with horizontal scale first, followed by vertical:

> Scale 1:1,000,000; vertical scale 6 times the horizontal.

Other models such as dolls, houses, and so forth, are entered under title, if recorded at all. The title is taken from the box or container; or, it may be supplied by the cataloger if there is no accompanying information. The word "(Model)" is added after the title. Collation includes the number of pieces and the size. If desirable, a note may be added to indicate possible use of the item.

Dioramas are scenes produced in three dimensions against an appropriate background. Entry is under the title, which is taken from the box or the item itself or supplied by the cataloger if no information is available. The term "(Diorama)" follows the title on the card, and the number of pieces forms the collation.

The term *Realia* is used to designate specific objects or specimens, such as a stone, a bird's egg, a cocoon, etc. These are entered under title or under name of the object, followed by "(Realia)." The number of pieces is given in the collation, and a note may be added to indicate exactly what is included if neither the title nor collation present all of the information.

Games and Kits

Games and Laboratory Kits are entered under title, which is taken from the box or accompanying information, or supplied by the cataloger. Following the title is the designation "(Game)" or "(Laboratory kit)," as appropriate. The number of pieces is given in the collation, and notes are added to indicate the purpose or use.

Multimedia Kits contain representations in more than one medium, and may or may not be designed for use as a unit. They may be treated in several ways: kept together as a set (particularly if intended for use as a unit), or separated with each medium treated independently. If the kits are kept together and entered

in a catalog or card file, entry is under title, followed by "(Kit)."
The collation includes the number of items in each medium—
for example:

1 filmstrip, 1 phonodisc, 2 pamphlets.

If the contents of the kit are separated, then each piece is entered
according to the rules for that type of material.

Maps and Charts

Maps come in many forms: small flat ones, folders (such as
travel and road maps), large flat maps, and wall maps. Maps rep-
resent subjects or geographic areas. The latter are more common
and are more likely to be in the collections of small libraries.
With geographic maps, the area covered is the important approach; therefore, it is recommended that maps be entered and
arranged under the area covered. (This is a break with the code
of the *Anglo-American Cataloging Rules*, which prescribes entry
under the person or corporate body primarily responsible for the
geographic content of the map.) Some libraries classify maps by
area as subject, using a preliminary symbol or letter, as M940
(Europe); others head them with the area covered and file them
in vertical files or map cases. Maps with class numbers are not
filed in the Pamphlet or Vertical File unless a separate drawer is
allocated for maps.

The larger and more important maps should be cataloged,
with the cards interfiled with others in the main catalog. The
cards can have colored edges, a plastic cover with color, or, preferably, the stamped designation "Map" above the call number.
The information given on the card is as follows:

1. Location symbol (e.g., M940, "Map," case and drawer
   number, or accession number—the accession number being a separate series from that for books)
2. The area (in capital letters as for any subject)
3. Title of the map
4. Publisher or issuing body
5. Date
6. Series, if part of one
7. Size (in inches)
8. Scale

A second card, identical with the catalog card (as illustrated in
Figure 20), is typed and filed in a separate section of the shelf list.
The map is stamped, marked with appropriate location symbol

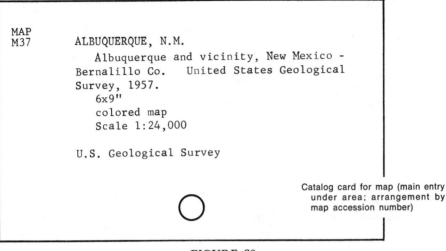

```
MAP
M37        ALBUQUERQUE, N.M.
              Albuquerque and vicinity, New Mexico -
           Bernalillo Co.    United States Geological
           Survey, 1957.
              6x9"
              colored map
              Scale 1:24,000


           U.S. Geological Survey
```

Catalog card for map (main entry under area; arrangement by map accession number)

FIGURE 20

(classification or "Map," or case number), and housed in a map case or cabinet drawer.

If not cataloged, the map is lettered like a pamphlet, with the area name as the subject, and is added to the vertical file folder.

Some small maps should be mounted on art paper or board; some large ones should be laminated or backed with cloth if they are to be much handled or folded. The practice of rolling them and standing them upright in an open case is not recommended.

A chart may be defined as a sheet presenting information in tables or diagrams. Charts are entered under the title followed by "(Chart)," with size given in the collation. They are usually housed in the Vertical File or in a map case.

Manuscripts, Letters, Archives, and Other Papers

Handwritten or typed materials occasionally become part of even a small library. Lesson plans, scripts, and other items may be part of the school library's teaching materials. A public library, because no one else is responsible, may become custodian of local history materials which include unpublished letters, speeches, reminiscences, or even official documents or records (archives) of organizations, firms, or government units. The church library could conceivably be the keeper of the church's official papers, sermons, etc.

These items may be classified by subject and kept in pamphlet boxes or verticle files, possibly separate ones; or some of them may be fully cataloged and classified.

For this type of material the librarian must often consult with others—the school librarian with his faculty, the church librarian with his clergy and church officials, and the public librarian with officials, archivists, and historical or research librarians—to determine use and protective measures.

Music

In general, music is cataloged according to the rules for cataloging books, the composer being considered the author. For an opera, musical comedy, or the like, the main entry is under the composer, with an author-title added entry under the librettist or person responsible for the nonmusical part of the work. If the nonmusical part is based on another work, this is explained in a note, and a reference may be made from this work to the composer and title of the item being cataloged.

```
Brahms, Johannes
   Academic festival overture for orchestra.
op.80. Foreword by Wilhelm Altmann.
Eulenburg, 1926.
   miniature score (56p.)   (Edition
Eulenburg, no.656)


   1   Overtures - Scores
```

Catalog card for music

FIGURE 21

A musical work, or a collection of works, whose artistic content is not attributable to an individual composer is entered under title or compiler as for nonmusical works. (See Chapter 3.)

If a library has a sizable collection of music (or anticipates one), it will be necessary to use uniform titles (see pages 51-53) for some works in order to bring all editions of a work together in the catalog.

The title pages of music frequently do not contain the kind of information usually found on the title pages of books. In such cases, the information is taken from the cover or caption title.

For music scores, the collation includes the designation "Score" and the number of parts, if more than one—for example:

score (32p.) and 3 parts

Unbound music, including sheet music, is most easily handled by arranging it according to composer, uncataloged, in flat drawers. Brief cards are prepared under composer's name followed by the name of the composition. On each card there should appear a record of the number of copies and the parts, etc. These cards may be kept in a separate file (in a public library) or in the catalog (in a school library) and stamped "Music," if that seems desirable. If the library has little music, records of holdings can be kept in the catalog. If, however, the library is custodian for an institution's choral, organ, orchestral and other performing music, separate records are better; the material is handled so much that its life is short and constant changing of catalog cards would be necessary.

Musical works, if bound or reinforced, must be carefully prepared so as to lie open and flat.

Periodicals, Newspapers, and Serials

A periodical is defined by the *A.L.A. Glossary of Library Terms* as "a publication with a distinctive title intended to appear in successive (usually unbound) numbers or parts at stated or regular intervals and, as a rule, for an indefinite time." Newspapers follow the same definition except that "their chief function is to disseminate news."

For either of these a checking card similar to the type shown in Figure 22 is used to enter each issue as it is received. These cards are available from library supply houses and may be obtained for different publication frequencies, such as daily, weekly, monthly, quarterly, etc. The record of receipt may be either a single check under the appropriate date or a notation of the number of the issue.

The magazines are stamped with ownership and arranged by title in a special section of the shelving. The current issues of at least the popular general and news magazines are displayed in a magazine section of special shelves or on a table in the reading room; the older ones are kept in special drawers or section of the stacks, arranged alphabetically by title. Those most valuable for reference use are kept for some years or as a permanent file; the

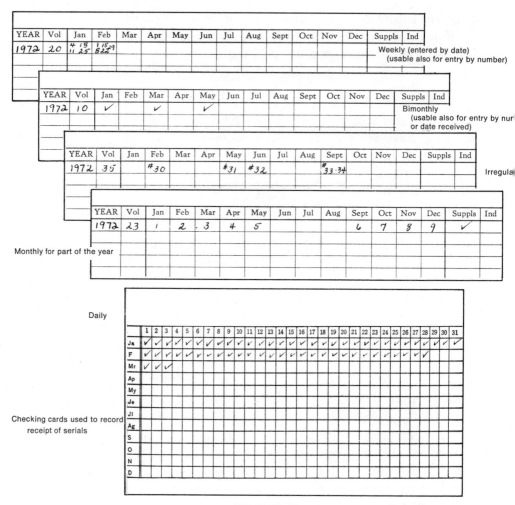

FIGURE 22

more ephemeral are discarded after their usefulness is past. If the individual issue is loaned out of the library, it will need strengthening; this can be done by placing it in a commercially made plastic cover or by pasting it into heavier covers. Those to be kept for longer reference use should be bound by a commercial library binding company, or they may be bound in the library by gluing issues of a completed volume together with plastic adhesive. (Materials for this work can be obtained from library supply houses.)

After magazines are bound or made into volumes, a record should be made on catalog cards arranged alphabetically in a special "Periodicals" section of the shelf list. Those which are bound and preserved may be cataloged and the cards interfiled in the card catalog, or in a separate "Periodicals" drawer. Some libraries prepare a list on sheets or strips in a visible file (available from library supply houses). Whatever method the library chooses to use—cards, a list, or a visible file—all periodicals received can be indicated and the library's holdings shown. For example:

> Time, v.20-   1945-   (Indicates the library has a file from 1945 and is still receiving it.)
>
> Vanity Fair, v.5-10. 1925-30; ceased publication. (Indicates the library has a file covering six years of a defunct periodical.)
>
> Jack and Jill (current issues) (Indicates that it is being received but not kept beyond the current year.)
>
> The Instructor, v.₍65-73. 1954-62.₎ (Indicates that the library has a broken file of scattered numbers for the years shown.)

Magazines are usually not classified by subject number; if the library is large enough or if there is a special use requiring classification, they may be arranged by a broad subject and kept near the books on related subjects, or in a special department. Thus, in a school, magazines dealing with educational methods, psychology, and related topics, may be kept in the teachers' professional collection. And a public library will keep magazines for children's use in the children's section.

Some publications other than magazines or newspapers are also published in serial form. These may be issued in numbered series or as annual publications. They may be monographic series (each a different work by a separate author) or true serials of nondistinctive authorship. Reports, proceedings, bulletins, and circulars are examples of serials. Monographic series may be kept as a set under the inclusive title, or they may be broken, with each individual monograph cataloged separately, placed in the vertical file, or treated like any other book or pamphlet. The nonmonographic serials are kept in sets. If important (local material in a public library, for example), the set may be cataloged (see page 61) or arranged by title with the magazines and used until it ceases to have any value. For serials not cataloged, checking cards should be made to indicate which issues have been received.

Paperbacks

A book to most people is one that is hard bound. Strictly speaking, the paperback is also a book since its contents are similar to (and often the same as) those of the bound book. But, because many paperbacks are of small size and fragile, they demand special consideration in the library.

Many paperbacks, particularly the "quality" books, which are printed on durable paper and issued and distributed by general publishers, are treated as are other books—classified, cataloged, accessioned, and prepared in the usual manner for circulation. To last long enough to justify this expensive treatment, however, most paperbacks must be given stronger backs. They can be acquired in so-called prebound library binding, they can be sent to a library binder, or they can be reinforced (strengthened). This is done by carefully removing the covers, pasting them to a heavier paper (such as "red-rope" or wallet), and then pasting them (with plastic adhesive) back on the book. Mylar covers are now available for paperback books; these provide some protection for the cover and spine, and they can be applied in much less time than is required for reinforcing. The lettering, pasting, and other preparations are then the same as for bound books.

Libraries (all kinds) also buy inexpensive paperbacks in quantities for lending. If processing costs can be kept down, many more people can be provided with these appealing books for curricular or extracurricular reading. The paper, binding, and margins are often so inadequate and the books themselves have frequently such a short life span that they do not justify the expensive treatment recommended above for the "quality" paper books. They should be purchased in lots—as many copies at one time as possible. They should not be cataloged, shelf listed, bound, or reinforced. They may be provided with an accession number for circulation use; a symbol may be part of the accession number: pb 1, pb 2, etc. Book cards and pockets can be prepared and inserted, books used until worn out, and then worn copies thrown away—there are no records to be corrected. The book card should give the last name of the author (as it is on the title page) and a short title of the work. Most libraries keep these books in one place, as in a display rack, although some prefer to interfile them with other books; but for nonfiction, the latter method involves checking them in the catalog and marking the class number on the spine or inside the book—and this adds to the cost.

Keeping Records Up to Date 15

Getting materials cataloged, organized, and into place is only part of maintaining a collection. New material comes in, and it may affect what is already there, or at least it must be fitted in with it. Books get damaged, wear out, are lost or stolen; this means records must be corrected.

Authority Records

Some libraries consider it necessary always to use the same form in the catalog for each personal and corporate name so that all cards for works by and about the person or body will file together. If the form of a name varies, references are made from unused forms to the one which is selected. (See Appendix I, pages 158-161, for examples of reference cards.)

To insure such consistent practice, an authority file of names is maintained. At one time such files were most elaborate, with cards indicating every reference work or "authority" which the cataloger consulted to "establish"—that is, find the fullest form of—the name. Such research is no longer done. It is actually necessary only to check the individual library's catalog to see if a name has been used and in what form, and to maintain a separate authority file only for those names which require cross references. This is done only to have a record of the references made so that they may be removed from the catalog when the name is no longer used. This record is best prepared on a 3 x 5 card with the name at the top as it appears in the catalog; the cross reference is typed below it, preceded by an "x," the accepted symbol for "refer from." (See Figure 23.)

If cards are made for selected items of information (such as analytics for works in certain series or illustrator cards for selected illustrators), records must be made and kept handy to the cataloging work. Decisions are made regarding individual serials: whether they are classed and cataloged; if so, whether as sets or

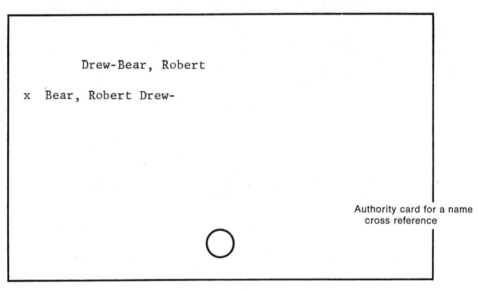

FIGURE 23

separately; whether analyzed; and so forth. These decisions may be recorded on the serials records, in a card list, or on the shelf-list card.

As was pointed out in Chapter 8, a list of classification or location symbols must be maintained to avoid duplication and to insure consistency in form. Until the library has a manual of cataloging practice, such decisions can be typed on sheets and kept in a loose-leaf notebook or on catalog cards filed in the work area.

For cataloging work done for a library in another place, as in a centralized processing center, records must be maintained at the center showing what subjects have been used and what cross references (subject or author) have been supplied to which libraries —or else the records must be kept at the individual libraries or branches and adjustments and references made there.

In other words, although record keeping should be kept to a minimum, any information which is necessary to doing the work properly should be recorded and kept available. Such records are necessary for consistency, and each library must decide where consistency is needed and to what extent.

The printed guides or tools will also serve as authority for what has been used and what is preferred practice. In the list of subject headings, checks may be used for subjects used and for cross references made (see the introductory chapter in the *Sears List*). When the last card under a subject is removed from the catalog, the list of subject headings must be consulted to see: (1) if any cross references should be removed, and (2) if there are "see also" references to be corrected. Finally, the checkings in the list are canceled. The library's decisions or preferences in regard to classification may be recorded in the schedules themselves. One disadvantage of making records in the printed tools instead of making card records is that when a new edition of a tool is acquired, the checking must be transferred to the new book, unless it is decided to use both the old and the new editions simultaneously. The latter practice is not recommended. The time spent in immediately transferring checks and notations from an old to a new edition of a printed tool is not wasted since much more time will be saved in the daily cataloging operation if only one edition is used. Transferring the notations, moreover, is an excellent means of acquiring an awareness of new subject headings and classification numbers.

Duplicates, Added Copies, Replacements, Continuations

So far as cataloging treatment is concerned, duplicates, added copies, and replacements are the same thing. It might be said that duplicates are additional copies of a title acquired at the same time as the first copy, added copies are copies acquired after the first one has been cataloged, and replacements are copies acquired to take the place of withdrawn ones.

No matter what it is called, each copy of a cataloged title is given an accession or copy number. The order record should show which books are added copies, and these should be handled separately from new titles. If the classification number is on the order record (as it should be), that leads directly to the shelf list and makes it unnecessary to check the catalog. The shelf-list card is withdrawn (in actual practice a group of books would be done at one time and all shelf-list cards for them pulled); the accession information is added to the card; a book card and pocket are typed; the shelf-list card is refiled immediately after work is revised; and the book is continued on its way. If there is likely to be some delay and if more than one person is going to be using the shelf list, a penciled dummy or (better) the order card, is left in place of the shelf-list card while it is out of the files. The duplicate or added-copy work can be done by a student assistant or clerk. Should a "duplicate" nonfiction book turn out to be a new edition, it requires new cataloging—a new set of cards for each edition.

For sets of books, annuals, etc., which are cataloged under an inclusive title, the added volumes (continuations) are processed in the same manner as added copies unless the new volumes cause a change in cataloging, such as changed author, editor, publisher, or title, in which case all the catalog cards may have to be withdrawn and changed. Sometimes the change means complete recataloging or reclassifying.

For "open entries" or continuations, sets, etc., the catalog cards may be changed to show the new additions. For instance, the number of volumes (which is penciled in) is changed to include the new volume, and the dates are changed to include the new accession. A contents note will need to be changed to show the new title. Some libraries make these changes only on the main entry card, stamping all the other cards to read: "For full information see entry under _____." When a set is completed or a serial ceases publication, the cards are all withdrawn and changed to include final information.

Recataloging and Reclassification

A certain amount of recataloging and reclassification is always to be expected. Terms go out of usage or change in meaning; new subjects come into existence and bring about changes in older ones; so much material may accumulate under a subject in the catalog or under one class number on the shelves that subdivision becomes necessary. Organizations, institutions, and people change their names or disclose real names. All of these things create the need for recataloging or connecting old and new by means of history cards or references. New editions of the classification scheme or the subject headings list or new codes and practices change meanings, groupings, interpretations, methods. The library must keep up with as many of these changes as possible, but should not jump at every suggested change without careful consideration and the conviction that the change is definitely needed to improve the service and provide for future consistency. Sometimes a change, particularly in subject headings or classification, is not adopted in a library because it involves "too much work"; later, the change must be made to avoid confusion and bring like things together. By the time this decision is finally made, more titles have been added and there are more items to be changed.

Innovations, independent revisions, adaptations, or altera-
tions of the printed tools should be scrupulously avoided. Today's improvisations too often create tomorrow's crises.

Withdrawals

A book is withdrawn from the collection when it is mutilated
or too worn or soiled to be usable; no longer useful (information
out of date, replaced by newer material, no longer read); lost in
circulation; shown to be missing through unfilled reserves or
searches; or missing in inventory. If it is a duplicate or a volume
in a set and there are other copies or volumes still in use, the catalog cards are not touched, but the accession information for the
missing volume is lined through on the shelf list. Some libraries
use different markings or colors to indicate different types of
withdrawal, e.g., ink for discarded volumes, pencil for missing
ones. (The theory here is that the discarded volume is physically
destroyed, but the missing one may reappear.)

If the missing volume is the only copy of the title or the last
one and not to be replaced, all catalog cards are withdrawn and
destroyed. The shelf-list card is also pulled but filed in a "discard" file. If the book is the last copy but is to be replaced, catalog
cards are left as they are and either the shelf-list card is flagged
with a colored metal clip and the date of order recorded, or else a
note is added to the order record stating that it is a last-copy replacement. Either process ensures the record's being cleared
eventually if the replacement never comes or if the publisher
sends a later edition. When this occurs, cards for the earlier edition are withdrawn and the new one is cataloged. When the book
to be withdrawn is in hand and is thus an actual discard, withdrawal procedures can be started at once; if it is missing, the records are not corrected for a year, during which time several
checks for the missing book are made.

Inventory

Library inventory, like any business inventory, is taking stock
of the property—in this case the book collection. Whether it is
done once a year, twice a year, once in five years, or not at all is
something to be decided according to the needs and institutional
requirements. If shelves are read often to keep the collection
fresh and if losses are few, the library may need inventories only
infrequently or not at all. If the losses are great, if books get
mixed up on the shelves, if the collection is small, or if the gov-

erning body so requires, frequent inventories may be needed.

If the charging system is one in which book cards are held by the library, inventory-taking is a simple process, and can be done for the various sections of the collection at different times. But if the charging is a photographic or transaction-card system, the process becomes more difficult, and it must be done all at one time when the library is closed to service.

The first step in taking inventory is to dismantle displays of books and to break up special collections, getting all classified books into their proper shelf-list order. The shelf-list drawer is then taken to the stacks, and the books on the shelves are checked against the cards. For each book found, a penciled symbol—letter or date—or a stamped notation is placed beside its accession information on the shelf-list card. Any card with unchecked numbers is turned on end—this can be done as reading progresses, or, if time is short at this stage, the shelf-list cards can be completely scanned later. Any book incorrectly marked or not matching the record in any way is laid aside for later correction. The shelf checking is preferably done by two people, one working with the shelf list and the other reading from the shelves. As many teams can work at one time as there are shelf-list drawers, people, and space.

After a drawer has been checked against the shelves, it is checked against the book cards for books in circulation. If the library uses photocharging, the checking may be done in one of two ways: (1) A group of people sit around a table, each with a shelf-list drawer, with another person reading the charge records from the film, the person concerned clearing the record in his drawer. (2) All books which are returned after the shelf-reading, over a period equivalent to the loan period, are checked against the shelf-list cards showing missing volumes. A little testing will show which method is less time consuming. After the process is completed, shelf-list cards still showing missing books are withdrawn, and a list is typed of the missing ones, giving call number, author's surname, brief title, accession or copy number. The books are searched for every three or four months; at the end of a year, those still missing are withdrawn from the records. The list of missing books is also gone over to consider replacement.

Statistics and Reports

Reports are necessary; they record history, show trends and developments, reveal accomplishments and needs, and are aids to public relations and publicity.

Statistics are needed to make reports; to show growth, work, services, and accomplishments; and to report to official statistics-gathering bodies. Statistics on cataloging may be divided into two groups—those showing the work done and those showing the holdings of the library. Both should be kept to a minimum and compiled only if they have real use or serve a real need. Probably any public library will want to ascertain the following:

Number of new titles added to adult and juvenile fiction collections

Number of titles withdrawn from adult and juvenile fiction collections

Number of new titles added to adult and juvenile nonfiction collections

Number of titles withdrawn from adult and juvenile nonfiction collections

Total number of volumes added to adult and juvenile fiction

Total number of volumes withdrawn from adult and juvenile fiction

Total number of volumes added to adult and juvenile nonfiction

Total number of volumes withdrawn from adult and juvenile nonfiction

Number of titles of periodicals received

Number of volumes of periodicals bound

Number of titles of newspapers received

Number of volumes of newspapers bound

Number of rolls of microfilm or sheets of microfiche added

Number of recordings added and withdrawn

Number of maps added and withdrawn

Number of films added and withdrawn

Number of slides added and withdrawn

Number of filmstrips added and withdrawn

Number of cassettes added and withdrawn

Number of phonotapes added and withdrawn

The counts of additions and withdrawals can be made on simple form slips as the work is done and then entered monthly in a statistics ledger or notebook. All of these figures will be added to or subtracted from the total library holdings in each category to show current stock; this is usually done annually.

School libraries will, of course, have fewer categories to record.

Another figure sometimes kept is the number of catalog cards prepared and filed; this counting is time-consuming and has little meaning unless withdrawn cards are also counted. A fair estimate of cards prepared can be made from the number of cards taken from stock or purchased. Some libraries also break book figures down by class number; this means extra work and should be done only if real need exists. If there seems no need to maintain separate statistics on fiction and nonfiction in a particular library, these counts can be combined. However, any breakdown used in recording statistics for additions must be followed in counting withdrawals.

There are certain "work" figures (as distinguished from "stock" figures) that libraries may wish to record. A list of examples follows:

Number of uncataloged paperbound books added
Number of pamphlets added
Number of pictures mounted and added
Number of books mended
Number of books rebound
Number of books jacketed with plastic covers

APPENDIXES

Directions for Typing

Outline

A. Equipment

B. Indentions

C. A catalog card and its parts

D. General typing practices

E. Typing the author card (main entry)

F. Typing a set of cards, using unit cards

G. Typing a complete set of cards

H. Changing (adapting) printed cards

I. Main entries other than author

J. Open entries

K. Analytics

L. Miscellaneous
   1. Conventional or form title
   2. Cross references
   3. History Cards
   4. Authority cards

M. Audio-visual and Other Nonbook materials
   1. Vertical file materials
   2. Maps
   3. Motion pictures
   4. Filmstrips
   5. Slides
   6. Phonodiscs

N. Shelf-list cards

O. Book cards and pockets

P. Abbreviations

Q. Some examples of shortened publishers' names

A. Equipment

1. *Typewriter* with elite or small gothic (plain, sans serif) type face

   Have keys changed on typewriter as needed, e.g., inferior brackets, accent marks (if there are books in foreign languages in the library), and script lower-case "l" (if needed) substituted for little-used keys.

   Use all-black ribbon.

   Keep keys clean so that letters won't clog.

2. *Prepared cards*

   Wilson, other printed or prepared cards

3. *Catalog cards*

   Use plain white (unlined) 3 x 5 cards from a library supply house.

4. *Erasers*

   Steel, knife-like eraser

   Typing eraser (pencil type)

   Small electric eraser if possible (cost: about $17)

5. *Heavy white thread* for tying cards together. (If more than one card is used for the same entry, cards are tied together by running the thread through the holes, tying over a pencil with square knot, and cutting thread about one third of an inch from knot.)

B. Indentions

   Set typewriter left-hand margin and tabular keys at proper indentions:

   Second space from left edge of card, for call number

   "First indention": 10 spaces from left edge of card

   "Second indention": 12 spaces from left edge of card

   "Third indention": 14 spaces from left edge of card

C. A catalog card and its parts.

```
Call        Author (main entry)
number        Title, including alternate title, editor,
            joint authors, etc.  Imprint  (publisher and
            copyright date)
              collation (paging or volume number)  (In
            parentheses:  series)


              Note
              2d note



              Tracings      ⭕
```

FIGURE 24

Each set of cards includes a main entry card, a shelf-list card and a card for each tracing.

D. General typing practices

1. *Strike-overs*

   Never strike one letter over another.

2. *Correcting errors*

   Single typing errors may be erased if this is done carefully, leaving no mark or torn surface; the correction must be in the exact spot of the letter or word removed.

3. *Spacing between items*

   Leave one space after words or names, commas, or semi-colons.

   Leave two spaces after colons or periods.

   Use single hyphen (no spaces) between dates (example: 1920-1935), for inclusive paging (example: 23-46) or other numerals, and in hyphenated words (example: so-called)

Leave one space for each digit of an incomplete number or date (example: 193 -19   )

Leave two spaces between different parts of the card (title, imprint, etc.)

Leave eight spaces to complete a name (example: Smith, J   Earl)

In a contents note, punctuate and space as indicated by cataloger; one preferred way is for each item to be followed by a period, one space, hyphen, one space, next item (example: Contents: The spy. - The fugitive. - The captive.)

In a subject heading, type dashes as space, hyphen, space (example: UNITED STATES - HISTORY)

4. *Spacing between lines*

Lines follow one another *except:*

Leave two lines between collation line and notes, and at least three lines between end of catalog information and tracings.

5. *Accent marks*

Type as written if the typewriter has accent marks; otherwise, add them with fine pen and black ink.

6. *Capitalization*

In general, follow practices of the language, i.e., in English capitalize proper names and words derived from proper names, titles of persons, historic events, first word of a sentence, or the beginning of a title of a book or other work.

In a title main entry, if the title begins with an article, the following word is also capitalized.

(Note: Older printed cards from LC or Wilson may have less capitalization; do not change printed cards, but do not follow their style in typing.)

For capitalization of standard cataloging abbreviations, follow practice as indicated on page 172.

7. *Punctuation*

In general, follow English usage.

Type copyright dates thus: c1963. (That is, type small "c" for copyright with no period and no space before date.)

Wherever possible, avoid using double punctuation, such as period and curve (parenthesis).

Follow punctuation in subject headings exactly as given.

(Note: On Wilson cards and in the Standard Catalog publications, rules for Wilson publications are followed. Thus, periods are omitted after imprint, in the collation, and at the end of the annotation. Space and period are omitted after abbreviations "p" and "v" when used with a numeral, as: 150p, v4, p73. Do not change printed cards, but do not follow this practice in typing cards.)

8. *Abbreviations*

Abbreviate standard terms as listed on page 172.

Abbreviate names of states following names of places (example: Chicago, Ill.)

Abbreviate names of countries following foreign places (example: London, Eng.)

E. Typing the author card (main entry)

1. *Call number*
Type the class (classification) number on the third line from top of card, two spaces from the left-hand edge of card.

Type the initial for the author's last name directly below class number. (If books are Cuttered, full work number appears here.)

Type additional parts of call number (such as date or volume number) directly below author initial.

Use no punctuation except for decimal in class number or period after "v."

Examples: | 940.54 | 808.3
| B | On6s
| 1963 | v.3

2. *Author's name (Figures 25 and 26)*

Type author's name at the first indention (10 spaces from left edge of card) on the third line from the top of the card.

Type last name first, followed by comma, one space, then first and middle names (if given), followed by comma, then dates (if used).

Type corporate names as written. If name runs over one line, drop to line below and begin at second indention.

```
National Society for the Study of Secondary
Education
```

FIGURE 25

If initials are used, do not follow them with periods.

Leave eight spaces after each initial.

If the main entry name is that of an editor, add "ed." after his name.

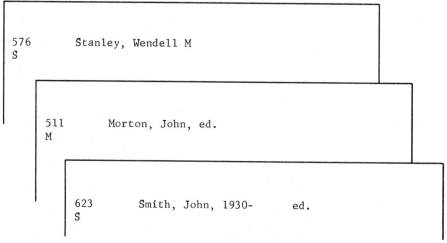

```
576        Stanley, Wendell M
S

511          Morton, John, ed.
M

623            Smith, John, 1930-        ed.
S
```

FIGURE 26

3. *The Title (Figures 27 and 28)*

Begin one line below the author's name, at second indention (12 spaces from left edge of card).

Information describing the book, such as authors, editors, edition, etc., is considered part of the title.

```
759.13        Guptill, Arthur L
                 Norman Rockwell, illustrator. Preface by
              Dorothy Canfield Fisher. Biographical
              introduction by Jack Alexander. 3d ed.
```

FIGURE 27

If an alternate title is shown, the short title is followed by a semicolon, the word "or," comma, and second title.

```
              Shakespeare, William
                 Florizel and Perdita; or, The winter's
              tale
```

FIGURE 28

If title transcription takes more than one line, continue on next line at first indention.

4. *Imprint* is the publishing information such as the publisher and date of publication or of copyright. *(Figure 29)*

This information follows two spaces after the title transcription, in the same paragraph (all lines after the first start at the first indention). Small "c" precedes the copyright date.

917.6   Horgan, Paul
H   The heroic triad; essays in the social
           energies of three Southwestern cultures.
           Holt, c1970.

FIGURE 29

5. *Collation* is the physical description of the book, including such information as number of pages, or number of volumes, whether illustrated, whether part of a series. *(Figure 30)*

Type this information one line below end of title paragraph, beginning at second indention.

The abbreviation "illus." follows two spaces after the paging, series (in parentheses) three spaces after paging or "illus."

No capitalization is used except for first word of series and for proper names.

Series note is in catalog entry form. (LC cards do not always do this; if using LC cards, do not change, but do not copy in typing.)

If series note runs over the line, return to first indention on next line.

```
National Bureau of Economic Research
   Economic forecasts and expectations;
analyses of forecasting behavior and
performance. Jacob Mincer, ed. c1969.
   251p. illus.   (National Bureau of
Economic Research.   Studies in business
cycles, 19)
```

```
Bosich, Joseph F
   Corrosion prevention for practicing
engineers. Barnes, c1970.
   250p. illus.   (Professional engineering
career development series)
```

FIGURE 30

6. *Notes* are sometimes added to explain history or content of the book. If used, notes follow two lines below the collation, starting at the second indention. *(Figures 31 and 32)*

They are given in paragraph form, each note beginning a new line at second indention and continuing at first indention if it runs over.

In a contents note, the items are usually followed by a period and dash (typed as space, hyphen, and space). They can, however, simply have commas or semicolons.

```
Brogan, Sir Denis William, 1900-
   Politics in America. Rev. ed., with a
new introd.  Harper, c1969.
   476p.

   London ed. has title: An introduction
to American politics.
   Bibliography: p.436-442.
```

```
DeNova, John A          comp.
   Selected readings in American history.
Contributing editors: Roger R. Trask, and
others.  Scribner, c1969.
   2 v.

   Contents. - v.1 Main themes to 1877. -
v.2 Main themes, 1865 to the present.
   Includes bibliography.
```

```
Brant, Irving, 1885-
   The fourth President, a life of James
Madison.    Bobbs, c1970.
   681p.

   A condensation of the author's 6v.
work entitled: James Madison; published
1941-61.
```

FIGURE 31

A bibliographical note may give the title of the bibliography (in quotes) or just the word "Bibliography," followed by a colon and the inclusive paging. Or it may say: Includes bibliographies (when there are several, appearing in different places).

```
920          Christopher, Maurine
               America's Black Congressmen.
             Crowell, 1971.
               283p. illus.

             Bibliography: p.270-273.
```

FIGURE 32

7. *Tracings* are indications of entries used on additional catalog cards. *(Figure 33)*

These may be arranged in paragraph form or in a column.

Type them at least three lines below the catalog information, at the first indention.

If there is not room on the face of the card, the card is turned and the items are typed near the bottom of the back of the card so that the card in the file can be tilted forward and easily read.

Tracings are numbered, with arabic numbers for subjects, roman for all others.

Tracings are typed on the main entry card and on the shelf-list card.

574   Hillcourt, William
H   The new field book of nature activities
        and hobbies; with 300 drawings and diagrams
        and 90 photographs; special project index of
        500 activities.   Rev.ed.   Putnam,1970.
           400p. illus.

           First published 1950 with title: Field
        book of nature activities. This edition
        has been revised.

        1 Nature study ◯   I Title

◯

        1 Nature study
        I Title

574   Hillcourt, William
H   The new field book of nature activities and hobbies; with
        300 drawings and diagrams and 90 photographs; special proj-
        ect index of 500 activities. ₍Rev. ed₎ Putnam 1970
        400p illus

            First published 1950 with title: Field book of nature activities. This
        edition has been ·revised
            Contains instructions for watching wildlife in the field, making nature
        collections and taking photographs. Projects dealing with various aspects
        of nature (such as soil and water conservation) are also described. Bib-
        liographies are included
        1 Nature study ɪ Title   574

        70W5495   ◯   (W) The H. W. Wilson Company

FIGURE 33

8. *Added cards ("run-on" or "second" cards) (Figure 34)*

If there is too much information to go on one catalog card, it is continued on a second card. Type at point of break, in parentheses: (Continued on next card)

On the second card, type the call number, the name of the author, the first two or three words of the title, three dots, the date, and a period; then, in parentheses: (Card 2). Two spaces below, type: Contents - Continued

```
Richards, Stanley.    Best plays of the
   sixties.   c1970.   (Card 2)

            Contents - Continued
George, by F. Marcus. - Hadrian VII, by
P. Luke. - The boys in the band, by
M. Crowley. - The great white hope, by
H. Sackler.
```

```
Richards, Stanley, 1918- comp.
   Best plays of the sixties.   Doubleday, c1970.
   1036p. ports.

   Contents. - Becket, by J. Anouilh. - The
night of the iguana, by T. Williams. -
Fiddler on the roof, by J. Stein, J. Bock,
and S. Harnick. - Philadelphia, here I
come, by B. Friel. - The odd couple, by

N.Simon. - The royal hunt of the sun,
by P. Shaffer. - The killing of Sister
```
                (Continued on next card)

FIGURE 34

9. *Grade or age level*

Some elementary school libraries or public libraries wish to show on catalog cards for children's books the appropriate age or grade level of the material.

This, if used, is typed in the upper right-hand corner of the cards.

10. *Use of stamps*

Some information which is used again and again, such as a word showing the type of material (map, filmstrip, slides, etc.) or a notation such as "Reference book," "Ask at desk," etc., can be stamped on, either above the call number (to show special materials or special shelving) or as a note.

F. Typing a set of cards, using unit cards

A set of cards includes the author card, a shelf-list card, and a card for each entry indicated in the tracings. If printed cards are used, all of the cards are just alike before typing, that is, like the main entry or author card.

1. *The main entry card*

One is left as it is (except for typing in the call number) and thus becomes the main entry card.

2. *Subject cards (Figures 35 and 36)*

If a tracing indicates that a subject card is to be made, the second card has typed at the top (one line above the author's name and at the second indention) the subject indicated in the first tracing.

This is typed all in capital letters and follows the form (punctuation, etc.) of the tracing, but with all words spelled out in full, except for standard abbreviations such as U.S.

If it is a long entry which will take more than one line, it is started at the second line above the author's name, and the run-on line starts directly below it, also at the second indention.

Dashes are typed as follows: space, hyphen, space (example: ROME - DESCRIPTION). A subject card is made for each subject indicated in the tracings.

The riddle of the Irish
914.15 **Molony, John Chartres,** 1877–
    The riddle of the Irish, by J. Chartres Molony. Port
Washington, N. Y., Kennikat Press ₍1970₎

    vii, 248 p. 19 cm. (Kennikat Press scholarly reprints. Series in
Irish history and culture)

IRELAND - SOCIAL LIFE AND CUSTOMS
914.15 **Molony, John Chartres,** 1877–
    The riddle of the Irish, by J. Chartres Molony. Port
Washington, N. Y., Kennikat Press ₍1970₎

    vii, 248 p. 19 cm. (Kennikat Press scholarly reprints. Series in
Irish history and culture)

IRELAND - POLITICS AND GOVERNMENT
914.15 **Molony, John Chartres,** 1877–
    The riddle of the Irish, by J. Chartres Molony. Port
Washington, N. Y., Kennikat Press ₍1970₎

    vii, 248 p. 19 cm. (Kennikat Press scholarly reprints. Series in
Irish history and culture)

IRISH QUESTION
914.15 **Molony, John Chartres,** 1877–
    The riddle of the Irish, by J. Chartres Molony. Port
Washington, N. Y., Kennikat Press ₍1970₎

    vii, 248 p. 19 cm. (Kennikat Press scholarly reprints. Series in
Irish history and culture)

914.15 **Molony, John Chartres,** 1877–
    The riddle of the Irish, by J. Chartres Molony. Port
Washington, N. Y., Kennikat Press ₍1970₎

    vii, 248 p. 19 cm. (Kennikat Press scholarly reprints. Series in
Irish history and culture)

    Reprint of the 1927 ed.

    1. Irish question. 2. Ireland — Politics and government. 3. Ire-
land—Social life and customs.   ɪ. Title.

DA950.M6 1970   914.15′03   74–102619
SBN 8046–0796–6   MARC

Library of Congress   70 ₍15–2₎

FIGURE 35

Wilson cards are available only with subjects and added entries printed on the cards. *(Figure 36)*

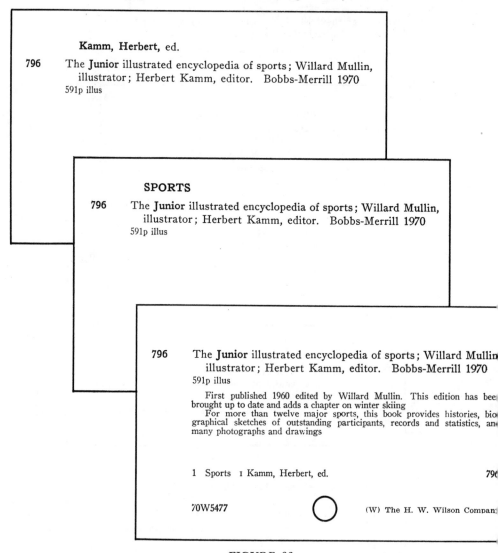

Kamm, Herbert, ed.

796 The **Junior** illustrated encyclopedia of sports; Willard Mullin, illustrator; Herbert Kamm, editor. Bobbs-Merrill 1970
591p illus

SPORTS

796 The **Junior** illustrated encyclopedia of sports; Willard Mullin, illustrator; Herbert Kamm, editor. Bobbs-Merrill 1970
591p illus

796 The **Junior** illustrated encyclopedia of sports; Willard Mullin, illustrator; Herbert Kamm, editor. Bobbs-Merrill 1970
591p illus

First published 1960 edited by Willard Mullin. This edition has been brought up to date and adds a chapter on winter skiing
For more than twelve major sports, this book provides histories, biographical sketches of outstanding participants, records and statistics, and many photographs and drawings

1 Sports ɪ Kamm, Herbert, ed. 796

70W5477   ◯ (W) The H. W. Wilson Company

FIGURE 36

3. Other added entries (Figure 37)

A card is made for other names indicated.

If one entry is designated "jt ed" or "ed," etc., that designation follows right after the name of the person so designated in the title position on the card.

Westby, Barbara M   ed.

025.33 **Sears** List of subject headings.   10th ed.   Ed. by Barbara M.
        Westby.   Wilson, H.W. 1972
        xlvi, 590p illus

    First published 1923 with title: List of subject headings for small libraries, by Minnie Earl Sears. In the 1972 edition, the editor has re-titled, rewritten and considerably enlarged the section: "Practical suggestions for the beginner in subject heading work;" she has also added numerous subjects which reflect current interest in social and environmental problems, while deleting outmoded and obsolete headings

   1   Subject headings   ɪ Westby, Barbara M   ed.   025.33

                (W) The H. W. Wilson Company

FIGURE 37

4. *Title entries (Figure 38)*

The word "Title" indicates that a title card is to be made.

On the line above the author's name, beginning at the second indention, type the title up to the first punctuation break.

If the title runs to a second line, start two lines above the author and continue on the next line at the third indention.

If a second title card is to be made the tracing will read: "Title: _____" (the part of the title to use). A title card is then made, just like the first except that only the part indicated is used.

```
                The states and the urban crisis
    309.2       The American Assembly
                The states and the urban crisis.
                Prentice-Hall, 1970.
                  215p.




          I  Title   II  Title: Urban crisis
```

```
                Urban crisis
    309.2       The American Assembly
                The states and the urban crisis.
                Prentice-Hall, 1970.
                  215p.




          I  Title   II  Title: Urban crisis
```

FIGURE 38

5. *Series entry (Figure 39)*

There may be a tracing for series, indicated by the word "series" or the word followed by a colon and the form of the series to be used.

Unless the form is indicated, the entry is made matching that in the series note on the card.

If it is a numbered series or includes a date, that information also is typed in the entry.

```
            The Reference shelf.  v.44, no.2
330.973   Nikolaieff, George A        ed.
            Stabilizing America's economy.  Wilson, 1972.
            256p.    (The Reference shelf. v.44, no.2)

            Bibliography:  p.245-56.




                            O
```

FIGURE 39

G. Typing a complete set of cards *(Figure 40)*

If all of the cards have to be typed, type only the main entry and shelf-list cards in full.

For each subject and added entry, prepare a shorter card. It carries, in addition to the added entry, the call number, the author's name in full, a short title, the publisher, and the date.

A short-form *title card* has only the call number, title at top, and the author's name.

H. Changing (adapting) printed cards.

Check the printed cards to be sure they match exactly the book being cataloged. The date may be different, or the publisher, the paging, or other detail.

If possible, change the cards by erasing the information which is wrong and typing in the corrected information. Tracings may be corrected by lining through unused parts.

If it will take more time to make all of the changes or if numerous changes will result in a messy card, type a new set of cards.

Place of publication, preliminary paging, size, etc., although not indicated usually, are left on printed cards since they don't give misinformation.

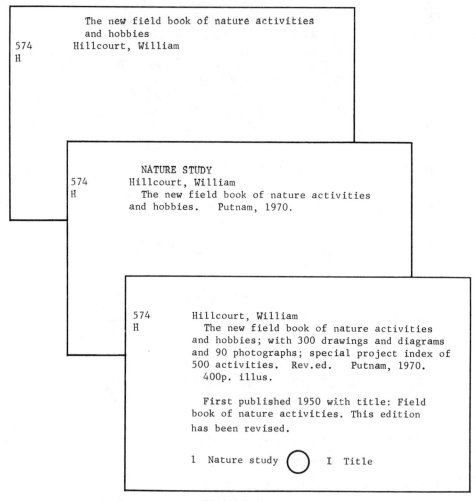

FIGURE 40

I. Main entries other than author

While most books are cataloged under the author's name, so that the main entry is the author's name, main entries can take other forms:

1. *Corporate name (Figure 41)*

A body or an organization may be responsible for the work; if so, the name of the group or organization appears in the place of the author's name. The card is otherwise the same. If the publisher is the same as the author, the name is not repeated in the imprint.

```
Committee for Economic Development
   Improving the public welfare system; a
statement by the Research and Policy
Committee.    1970.
   75p.
```

FIGURE 41

2. *Title entry (Figure 42)*

For periodicals and other serials without an author, the title is the main entry.

When the author is not known or there are many authors, the title is used as the main entry.

For title main entry cards, the title begins at the first indention, and all other lines, down to the notes, begin at the second indention. This is called "hanging indention."

```
Sears List of subject headings. 10th ed.
   Ed. by Barbara M.Westby.    Wilson, 1972.
   590p. illus.
```

FIGURE 42

3. *Set of books (Figure 43)*

Sometimes a set of books is cataloged as a set. If there is no author or there are many authors, the set is cataloged by title and hanging indention is used.

```
503       McGraw-Hill Encyclopedia of science and
M            technology; an international reference
             work in fifteen volumes including an
             index.    McGraw, 1971.
             15v. illus., maps.
```

FIGURE 43

Note that the first word of the distinctive title (Encyclopedia) is capitalized.

(Nonbook materials have special rules for cataloging and typing; see M, Audio-visual and Other Nonbook Materials, pages 163-167).

J. Open entries *(Figure 44)*

Periodicals and other serials, certain reference books, and other works are not published all at once, but are received volume by volume.

These are cataloged when the first volume arrives, but since all of the information is not available then, the entry has to be left "open," that is, for final information to be supplied later.

Some of these are under title, hence typed with hanging indention.

Some have authors.

The date of the earliest volume is given in the usual place for date and is followed by a hyphen. (After the set is complete, the date of the last volume is filled in and closed with a period.)

In place of paging, two spaces are left and then a "v" is added.

After a set is complete, the number of volumes is inserted.

A series note may be included; this also is left open, thus:
(The Genealogical Society. Papers, no.6, 8

(Note that there is no punctuation after the 8, and the parentheses are not closed.)

The Best short plays. 1937–
  ₍Philadelphia, Chilton Book Co.₎

    v. 21 cm. annual.

   Suspended 1961–67.
   Title varies: 1937–1951/52, The Best one-act plays.
   Founded and edited for some years by M. Mayorga.
   Imprint varies: 1937–1954/55, New York, Dodd, Mead.—1955/56–
  1960/61, Boston, Beacon Press.

```
Adams, James Truslow, 1878-1949
   The march of democracy; a history of the
United States.   Scribner's, 1965-
      v.

   Contents. - v.1 The rise of the Union. -
v.2. A half-century of expansion. - v.3.
Civil War and aftermath.
```

FIGURE 44

The information may be "closed" with each volume by changing in pencil the details of the latest volume received, thus: v.1-(3), 1961-(1963), (3)v. (The information in parentheses would be in pencil until the set is completed.) If this is done, work can be saved by keeping these records up to date only on the main entry card and stamping all the other cards with a note reading: "For full information see Main Entry."

K. Analytics *(Figures 45 and 46)*

A section of a work, a part of a book, or a volume of a set is sometimes important enough to be looked for separately, in which case an extra card is made to locate it. Such entries are

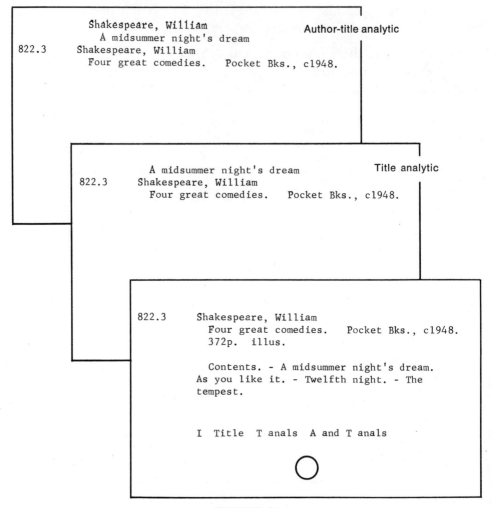

FIGURE 45

called analytics, and there are several kinds: author analytics, title analytics, subject analytics, author and title analytics, and title and author analytics.

With unit cards, these are prepared by typing the additional information above the main entry.

Single-line analytical entries are typed one line above the main entry at the second indention.

Two-line author and title entries are typed in the two lines above the main entry at the second and third indentions; title and author entries are typed at third and second indentions.

If cards are all being typed, a shortened form may be used, giving, besides the analytical entry, the call number, the author in full, a shortened title, the publisher, and the date.

Analytics are indicated in the tracings with the abbreviation "anal" followed, if necessary, by a colon and the entry for the analytic.

If the full card carries a contents note and all items in the contents are to be analyzed, one or two tracings may indicate all.

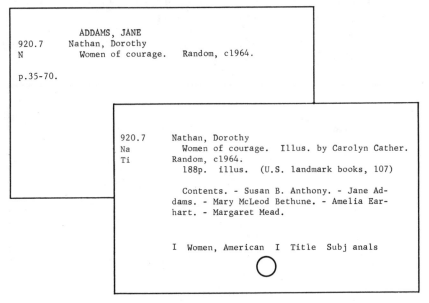

FIGURE 46

Thus, "a anals" indicates that every author listed in the contents is to have a card for his name. If the tracing says "a and t anals," two-line author and title entries are used for all works listed; "t and a anals" indicates two-line title and author entries for all works.

Subjects and subject analytics are always traced in full—for example, "anal: GEOLOGY."

On occasion an analytic (particularly a subject analytic) is indicated for a section of the book and this is not made clear on the face of the card. Then the paging is given, this paging typed at the left side of the card, two spaces below the call number. The paging is indicated in the tracing: "anal: GEOLOGY. p. 180-226."

L. Miscellaneous

1. *Uniform title (Figure 47)*

If the work being cataloged is published under different titles or variations, a "uniform" or "conventional" title may be adopted in order to bring all of the variations together in the catalog.

The uniform title is typed in the place where the title usually appears (second indention, one line below the author's name) and is enclosed within brackets.

The real or title-page title follows on the line below, also starting at the second indention.

```
Shakespeare, William, 1564-1616
  [Hamlet]
  The tragedy of Hamlet, Prince of Denmark,
ed. by George Lyman Kittredge. Rev. by
Irving Rebner, Blaisdell, c1967.
    179p.    (The Kittredge Shakespeares)
```

FIGURE 47

2. *Cross references (Figure 48)*

Cards are typed to refer users from terms or names not used (or in a different spelling) to those which are in the catalog.

These are cross references, called *"see" references.*

The form of the card is as follows: The term not used is at the top line (i.e., third line from the top of the card) at the second indention.

Two lines below and at the third indention appears the word "see" (not capitalized).

Two lines below this and at the first indention is the term or name which is used.

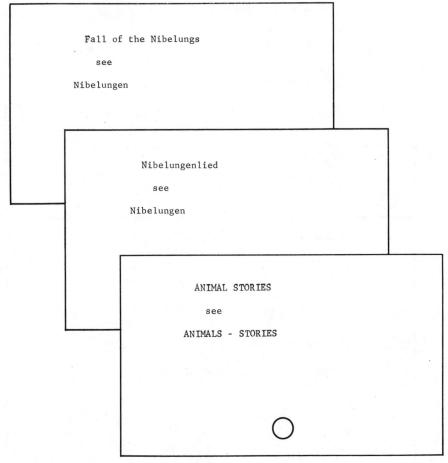

FIGURE 48

References are also made from terms which are used to other related terms which may be helpful to the reader. These are called *"see also" references*, since "see also" is used instead of "see" on reference card. They are most often used for subjects. *(Figure 49)*

They are typed in a form similar to that for "see" references.

When several terms are referred to, they are typed alphabetically, one below the other.

If subjects, the terms are all in capital letters.

```
        ANIMALS - STORIES

           see also

   ANIMALS - HABITS AND BEHAVIOR
   ANIMALS IN LITERATURE
   FABLES
     also names of special animals with the
        subdivision STORIES, e.g.
     DOGS - STORIES
```

```
        ANIMALS IN LITERATURE

           see also

   ANIMALS - POETRY
   ANIMALS - STORIES
   BIBLE - NATURAL HISTORY
     also BIRDS IN LITERATURE; and
        similar headings
```

FIGURE 49

3. *History cards (Figure 50)*

People change their names or write under different names; organizations and other bodies may also change names.

The practice is to catalog under the name used in the book being cataloged, and to pull the various forms together by means of "history cards."

These may be in the form of a paragraph of explanatory text or in a form resembling "see also" cross references.

Creasey, John

    The works of this author have been pub-
lished under the following names, where they
will be found in this catalog:

Ashe, Gordon
Creasey, John
Halliday, Michael

Hunt, Kyle
Marric, J.J.
Morton, Anthony
York, Jeremy

        Creasey, John

            see also

        Ashe, Gordon
        Halliday, Michael
        Hunt, Kyle
        Marric, J. J.
        Morton, Anthony

        York, Jeremy

        National Association for the Study and
            Prevention of Tuberculosis

                For works by this body issued
                under its later name see

        National Tuberculosis Association

FIGURE 50

4. *Authority cards (Figure 51)*

Records must be kept to indicate what references have been made.

The information is recorded on cards, but these cards are not filed in the catalog; they are kept in a separate "authority file" in the cataloging area. All authority cards are in one file.

The authority card for a "see" reference has as entry the name or term under which cards are filed in the catalog.

Three lines below are listed the names or words under which references have been made. In front of each is a small "x," the symbol for a "see" reference.

If the library has more than one public card catalog, the authority card shows in which catalog or catalogs the reference appears. This is done by means of a symbol for the catalog following the term from which a cross reference is made. Thus on an authority card headed Shakespeare, William, the notation "x Shakspere (a" means that a reference appears in the adult catalog referring the reader from "Shakspere" to the heading used.

Nibelungen

x Nibelungenlied (a.j
x Fall of the Nibelungs (a.j

FIGURE 51

For every history card appearing in the catalog, a card just like it is made for the authority file; if the library has more than one catalog, the history authority card indicates in which catalog the term appears.

Whenever a *see also* card is made, a duplicate must be made for the authority file, indicating, if necessary, in which catalog it appears. Exception: authority cards need not be made for subjects taken from the subject headings list; records for these (including the catalogs in which they are used) are made in the headings list itself.

M. Audio-visual and Other Nonbook Materials

The typing of cards for the nonbook materials differs little from the typing of cards for books. The format of the card is the same: if the main entry is under author, the author's name is typed at the first indention, and the title begins at the second indention; when main entry is under title, the title begins at the first indention, runs over to second indention, and remains there through the imprint (see page 153).

The main difference in cards for nonbook materials is in the collation, where instead of pages or volumes one types reels, frames, slides, prints, pieces, sides, etc., as appropriate to the type of material represented by the card. The directions for cataloging these materials indicate the order in which the information appears on the catalog card. (See Chapter 14.)

1. *Vertical file materials* (pamphlets, pictures, clippings, maps, etc. kept in a vertical file)

One card is typed with the subject on it. If the index to the vertical file material is a separate one, this is all that needs to be done. If the card is to be filed in the catalog, more information is required (see Figure 52).

LABOR AND LABORING CLASSES

Additional material on this subject
will be found in the Vertical File.

FIGURE 52

2. *Maps*

For cataloged maps, the word "Map" is stamped or typed in the upper left-hand corner of the catalog card.

Directly below will be the map number.

On the same line (where the author's name appears on a book catalog card), at the first indention, the subject (i.e, the area covered) is typed (in capital letters).

On the lines below, all at the second indention, are typed the other cataloging data: title, publisher and date, issuing body, series, scale, size, etc. (Any item running over one line carries to the first indention on the second line.) (See Chapter 14, Figure 20.)

3. *Motion pictures*

The words "Motion picture" are stamped or typed in upper left corner of the card, with the accession number below it in call-number position.

The title appears in the place of the author; this is followed by the other information in paragraph form, with hanging indention: producer, date, number of reels (if more than one), running time, indication of sound track, color or black-and-white notation, size, series note. Additional notes are added as needed, in paragraph (regular note) form.

Tracings also follow same pattern as for books. (See Chapter 14, Figure 17.)

4. *Filmstrips (Figure 53)*

Cards are typed for individual titles in the same manner as those for films, and the word "Filmstrip" is stamped or typed in the upper left-hand corner.

```
Filmstrip
FS25        The Christmas story (Filmstrip)
               Museum Extension Service,
               1955.
               40 fr. col.

               Summary: Renaissance paintings from the
            collection of the National Gallery of Art
            are arranged to illustrate the story of
            the birth of Christ.
```

FIGURE 53

5. *Slides*

Slides are generally entered under title, and the word "Slide" and the accession number are typed in the upper left corner of the card.

The collation gives the number of slides and the size.

Any necessary notes are typed in the usual position for notes. (See Chapter 14, Figure 18.)

6. *Phonodiscs (Figures 54 and 55)*

The catalog cards carry the designation "Phonodisc" and the accession number in upper left corner.

For musical recordings, the main entry is under composer, or title if it is a collective recording. If there are several separate works on one disc, each is cataloged with separate cards. Notes and tracings are given as for other types of material.

```
Phonodisc
Disc 102  Folk songs of the Old World (Phonodisc)
             Capitol PBR8345.
             4s.  12in.  33 1/3 rpm.


             Roger Wagner Chorale; Roger Wagner,
          conductor.



             1  Folk-songs  I  Roger Wagner Chorale
```

```
Phonodisc
Disc 81   Bach, Johann Sebastian
             ⌜Inventions, harpsichord⌝ (Phonodisc)
             Two-and three-part inventions.    Vox
          PL10,550.
             2s  12in.  33 1/3 rpm.

             Alexander Borovsky, piano.

             1  Canons, fugues, etc. (Harpsichord)
          I  Borovsky, Alexander
```

FIGURE 54

Nonmusical recordings are entered under author if there is one, or title if there is no single author.

The designation "Phonodisc" and accession number are typed in the upper left corner.

```
Phonodisc
Disc 95    Hughes, Langston
              The poetry of Langston Hughes
           (Phonodisc)   Caedmon TC1272.
              2s.  12in.   33 1/3 rpm. microgroove


           Read by Ruby Dee and Ossie Davis.



           I  Dee, Ruby   II  Davis, Ossie
```

FIGURE 55

N. Shelf-list cards *(Figures 56-A and 56-B)*

The shelf-list card is an exact copy of the main entry card in-cluding the tracings—for all types of material. (Some older Wilson cards supply shorter form; on these, at least the trac-ings should be added.)

In addition, the shelf-list card has a record of the number of volumes and number of copies of the title held by the library.

For the public library, price (whatever is charged for a lost book) is given following the accession or copy number. (Schools do not need this.)

If there is room on the front of the card, this accession infor-mation is typed there; if not, the card is flipped and the back is used. (The card is placed in the typewriter with the face of the card showing and the card right side up; when it is rolled into place, the typing on the back then runs in the opposite direction from the face and thus is easier to read when filed.)

As little punctuation as necessary is used.

```
jF          Stevenson, Robert Louis
               Treasure Island.   World


            I  Title

copy 1  2.00 (Falls illus)
copy 2  2.25 (Doubleday. Wyeth illus)
```

341.13 Eichelberger, Clark M
      UN: the first twenty-five years.   Harper & Row 1970
178p

    First published 1955 as: UN: the first ten years, and revised at five year intervals
    The author "sketches the history of the United Nations and evaluates its current strengths and weaknesses and his hope for its future." Publisher's note

70-21 5.95
71-56 5.95

    1 United Nations   ɪ Title   341.13

70W5478   (W) The H. W. Wilson Company

FIGURE 56-A

R
920
W

Who's who in America; a biographical dictionary of **notable** living men and women of the United States. . . Marquis 1899-

v

"Issued biennially; first edition 1899
"An excellent dictionary of contemporary biography containing concise biographical data, with addresses and, in case of **authors, lists** of works." Mudge

1   U.S.—Biography—Dictionaries   920.03

63W12,665   O   (W)   The H. W. Wilson Company

O

1958   8.00

~~1960 12.00~~
1961   15.00

1963   22.00
1961   cop 2 12.00

FIGURE 56-B

A shelf-list card for a biography is made to match the subject card rather than the author card—that is, the name of the subject of the book is put at the top, for the biography cards are arranged by subject in the shelf list.

For fiction and easy picture books, one shelf-list card is used for all editions. After the accession number the variation is shown, e.g., publisher, illustrator. (See Figure 56-A, first card.)

O. Book cards and pockets *(Figures 57-A and 57-B)*

On the book card appear the call number, the last name of the author, a short title, volume number if necessary, copy or accession number, and, sometimes for a public library, the price.

If there is no author, the form of the main entry is followed, even to hanging indention.

The book pocket carries only the call number and accession number.

For books not classified, the author's last name and a short title are added to the pocket.

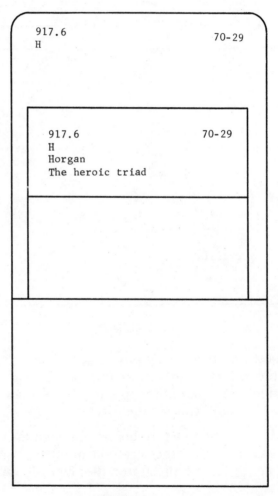

FIGURE 57-A

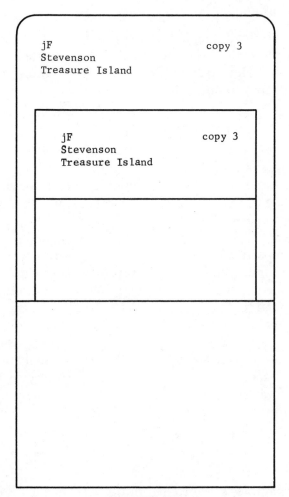

FIGURE 57-B

(The information on the card is to identify the individual volume or piece while in circulation; the information on the pocket is to check quickly the identifying information with the book card.)

Book cards are not made for noncirculating materials such as reference books, bound periodicals, microfilms, etc.

P. Abbreviations

Certain abbreviations are standard usage on catalog and book cards. (These do not include abbreviations used in tracings, which are primarily for librarians' use.) Among those used generally are the following:

abr.	abridged	pt. (pts.)	part(s)
&	and (used in publisher's name)	pref.	preface
		Pr.	press (in publisher's name)
assoc.	association, associated	pseud.	pseudonym
bk.	book	pub.	publisher, published, publication
Co.	company		
c	copyright	rev.	revised (as edition)
dept.	department	ser.	series
ed.	edited, editor, edition	suppl.	supplement, supplemented, supplements
enl.	enlarged		
illus.	illustrations, illustrated, illustrator	tr.	translator, translation, translated
introd.	introduced, introduction	U.S.	United States
		Univ.	university (publisher)
n.d.	no date		
no. (nos.)	number(s)	v.	volume, volumes
p.	page, pages		

Q. Some examples of shortened publishers' names

Allyn	Allyn & Bacon, Inc.
Am. Bk.	American Book Company
A.L.A.	American Library Association
Appleton	Appleton-Century-Crofts
Arco	Arco Publishing Company, Inc.
Assoc. Pr.	Association Press
Atheneum	Atheneum Publishers
Beacon Pr.	Beacon Press
Bowker	R. R. Bowker Company
Cambridge	Cambridge University Press
Chilton	Chilton Book Company
Collier	P. F. Collier, Inc.
Coward	Coward-McCann & Geoghegan, Inc.

Crowell	Thomas Y. Crowell Company
Crowell Collier	Crowell Collier and Macmillan, Inc.
Doubleday	Doubleday & Company, Inc.
Dutton	E. P. Dutton & Company, Inc.
Farrar, Straus	Farrar, Straus & Giroux, Inc.
Grosset	Grosset & Dunlap, Inc.
Grove	Grove Press, Inc.
Harcourt	Harcourt Brace Jovanovich, Inc.
Harper	Harper & Row, Publishers
Heath	D. C. Heath & Company
Holt	Holt, Rinehart and Winston, Inc.
Houghton	Houghton Mifflin Company
Knopf	Alfred A. Knopf, Inc.
Little	Little, Brown & Company
McGraw	McGraw-Hill Book Company
Morrow	William Morrow & Company, Inc.
Oxford	Oxford University Press, Inc.
Oxford Bk.	Oxford Book Company, Inc.
Praeger	Praeger Publishers, Inc.
Prentice-Hall	Prentice-Hall, Inc.
Rand McNally	Rand McNally & Company
Random	Random House, Inc.
Regnery	Henry Regnery Company
Revell	Fleming H. Revell Company
Scott	Scott, Foresman and Company
Scribner	Charles Scribner's Sons
Univ. of Calif. Pr.	University of California Press
Watson-Guptill	Watson-Guptill Publications
Watts	Franklin Watts, Inc.
Wiley	John Wiley & Sons, Inc.
Wilson	The H. W. Wilson Company
World Pub.	World Publishing Company

Rules for Alphabetical Filing in a Small Dictionary Catalog

The following rules were compiled by the author of the first edition after studying many sets of rules, published and unpublished, and after talking to many people regarding practices and preferences. A few are innovations and depart from established practice for the sake of logic and consistency. Among these are Rule 12, recommended by school librarians, reference librarians, and others as following the primary rule (file as written) and following telephone book practice, with which library patrons are familiar; Rule 14a, according to which all entries for an author's works are arranged alphabetically, with collective titles such as *Works* included in the alphabetical sequence instead of being grouped before individual titles; and Rule 14g, which prescribes consistent chronological order even for editions of the same work. The rules have been retained, with minor revisions, in the present edition.

1. Arrange the catalog cards alphabetically by the first word or name appearing at the top of the card, i.e., "the entry," disregarding a beginning article.

2. File word by word rather than letter by letter. A one-word entry comes before the word followed by succeeding words.

   Royal
   Royal personages
   Royal, Sydney
   Royalle, Guy
   Royalty

3. File all entries alphabetically, by first term, then by second, then third, etc., regardless of form of entry—names or words, main entry or added entry, author or subject or other type, forename or surname.

> The house *(title)*
> House and garden *(periodical title)*
> House, Boye *(author or added entry)*
> HOUSE CLEANING *(subject)*
> The house party *(title)*
> House, William *(name)*
> House with roots *(title)*
> Household, Geoffrey *(name)*

4. Disregard articles, in English and foreign languages, at the beginning of an entry, but take them into account elsewhere. All other words, including prepositions and pronouns, are considered in filing.

> The best in American cooking
> Best plays of the sixties
> Economic concepts
> An economic detour
> Especially ocelots
> La espera
> For life and liberty
> Il garzella
> Miracles in dispute
> Les misérables

5. File abbreviations (e.g., *Mr., Dr., St., U.S.*) as though spelled out (*Mister, Doctor, Saint* or *Street, United States*), except *Mrs.* which is filed as written. The figure *&* is filed as *and.*

6. A letter, single-letter word, or initial is filed at the beginning of the letter before words beginning with that letter.

> ABC about collecting
> ABC's of dance terminology
> AB papers
> ACTH
> The a cappella chorus
> AE's letters
> A is for angel
> A.L.A.
> The A to Z of poodles
> A-V bibliography
> Aaburg, Charles

7. Arrange acronyms (brief forms of corporate names or terms made up of groups of letters commonly written and spoken as words) as words, unless written in all capitals with periods or spaces between the letters.

Asimov, Isaac
Aslib. Cranfield Research Project
Aslin, Elizabeth
Forten, Charlotte
FORTRAN (COMPUTER PROGRAM LANGUAGE)
Fortune and men's eyes
Unemployed
UNESCO bibliographical handbooks
Unesco manuals for libraries

8. Numerals and dates in headings are filed as though spelled out and as customarily spoken in English; thus "1905" is filed as "Nineteen five"; "1,000" as "one thousand."

One
1 and 2 make 3
100
One million
1000

9. Accents and other diacritical marks and punctuation are ignored in filing. This includes an apostrophe showing possession, a plural, or an elision. Thus, "ä" is filed as "a"; "ç" as "c." Parentheses are also ignored.

Dogs follow John
The dog's following Mary
A dog's life
GEOLOGY
GEOLOGY AS A PROFESSION
Geology as a science
GEOLOGY, ECONOMIC
GEOLOGY—NEW YORK
GEOLOGY—WEST VIRGINIA

10. Hyphenated words are considered two separate words if the part preceding the hyphen can stand alone, but as one word if the part preceding the hyphen is dependent. (In case of doubt, follow the practice of a selected unabridged dictionary.)

The machine for tomorrow
Machine-sorted cards
Machinery

But:

The producer
Pro-European viewpoints

11. Words spelled or written two or more ways are interfiled in one place, with references from the form not used. (In deciding, follow a selected unabridged dictionary.)

Base ball	see	Baseball
Catalogue	see	Catalog
Labour	see	Labor

12. Names (including those beginning *Mac, Mc*, etc.) are always filed as written, no matter how pronounced or how close to other forms. (Allen or Allan, Smith or Smyth.)

Brown, John
Brown Mountain
Brown, Robert
Browne, Amos

Machinery
MacPherson
McBain
McMahon
M'Gregor

13. For forenames used by several people, follow the alphabetic arrangement if possible; if a descriptive phrase is needed, the phrase is employed alphabetically. For royalty, popes, etc., the numeral is ignored unless all other designation is the same for two or more people, in which case the arrangement becomes chronological, earliest first.

Charles	*(title of work)*
Charles, A. Aldo	*(surname)*
Charles A. Coffin Foundation	*(corporate name)*
Charles and Cromwell	*(title of work)*
Charles, count of Flanders	*(forename)*
Charles County, Md.	*(place name)*
Charles d' Orleans	*(forename with title)*
Charles I, emperor of Germany	*(forename)*
Charles IV, emperor of Germany	(")
Charles V, emperor of Germany	(")
Charles IV, king of France	(")
Charles I, king of Great Britain	(")
Charles II, king of Great Britain	(")
Charles I, king of Spain	(")
Charles of Sessa	(")
Charles-Picard, Colette	*(hyphenated surname)*

Charles R. Walgreen Foundation	*(corporate name)*
Charles River, Mass.	*(place name)*
Charles the Good	*(forename and appellative)*
Charles W. Eliot and popular education	*(title of work)*

14. For entries under an author:
    a. File by the title of the work with which the person is associated whether name is main entry or secondary.
    b. If the person is an added entry, the card is next filed by the title of the work, disregarding main entry.
    c. If the same work appears both as title of a book and title of an analytic, file title of the book first.
    d. If the entry is for author and title analytic, the card is filed by author, then title, then main entry.
    e. File subject cards about an individual after all of the works *by* him. File second by the author of the book, and third by title.
    f. File a criticism of a *work* following the entry for the work.
    g. File editions of the same work chronologically by date or number (earliest first), those with no number or date before the others.

Dickens, Charles   *(author and title of book)*
  Bleak House

Dickens, Charles   *(author and title analytic)*
  Bleak House
Dickens, Charles
  Collected works

Dickens, Charles   *(author and uniform title)*
  ₍A Christmas Carol₎
  The Christmas story, a Christmas Carol

Dickens, Charles   *(author and title analytic)*
  A Christmas Carol
Leverton, Garrett
  Plays for the College theatre

DICKENS, CHARLES   *(subject criticism of a title)*
  A CHRISTMAS CAROL
Jacques, Edward
  Dickens' Christmas Carol

Dickens, Charles
    Collected works

    Dickens, Charles, ed.   *(added entry)*
Collins, Wilkie
    Under the management of Mr. Charles Dickens; his production of "The frozen deep"

Dickens, Charles
    The wreck of the Golden Mary

    DICKENS, CHARLES   *(subject)*
Adrian, Arthur
    Georgian Hogarth

    DICKENS, CHARLES   *(subject)*
Fawcett, Frank D
    Dickens the dramatist

15. If the same title appears as an entry word more than once, it is sub-arranged by author; if it is the same work, it is further sub-arranged by date of publication, earliest first. If the same title appears as a title of a periodical and another work, the periodical comes first; if the title entry for the same work appears as both the title of an anlytic and a book, the book comes first.

House beautiful; a monthly magazine   *(title of periodical)*

    House beautiful   *(title of book)*
Jones, Adam
    House beautiful

    House beautiful   *(title analytic)*
Jones, Adam
    Collected stories

16. For subject entries arrange in order:
    a. Subject without subdivision, arranged by main entry.
    b. Date and period subdivision, chronologically arranged, earliest first, and most inclusive period before shorter periods within the inclusive period, e.g., U.S. - HISTORY - 20TH CENTURY; U.S. - HISTORY - 1900-1914.

c. Other subdivisions alphabetically.

U.S.—DESCRIPTION
U.S.—HISTORY
U.S.—HISTORY—DISCOVERY AND EXPLORATION
U.S.—HISTORY—COLONIAL PERIOD
U.S.—HISTORY—CIVIL WAR
U.S.—HISTORY—20TH CENTURY
U.S.—HISTORY—1900-1914
U.S.—HISTORY—BIBLIOGRAPHY
U.S.—HISTORY, NAVAL
U.S.—HISTORY—PERIODICALS

17. File a "see also" reference or a history card (explaining change of name, etc.) following all of the entries for the same word or phrase or name.

Library Terminology as Used in This Book

Accession—A book or other library item acquired as part of a library's collections or holdings; *to accession* is to assign an identifying and sequential number to each item added to the library's collection.

Accession Number—A number assigned each book or other item, in order of its receipt in the library.

Added Copy—A copy, other than the first, of a book or other material; a duplicate.

Added Entry—A catalog entry (see *Entry*) other than the main or subject entry; added entries may be titles, joint authors, series, etc.

Added Volume—A volume of a set of books or a serial other than the first; a continuation.

Analytic—A catalog entry for a part of a book or work. There are author, title, subject, series, author and title, and title and author analytics.

Annotation—A brief description of the contents of a book, subject matter of a film, etc.

Annual—A work published every year, such as annual report, proceedings, yearbook.

Anonymous—Applied to a work published without indication of the author.

Anonymous Classic—A literary work whose authorship is lost in history, such as a folk epic, folk story.

Audiodisc—See *Phonodisc.*

Author—The person or corporate body responsible for the creation of a book or other work.

Author Analytic—A catalog entry, identifying the author of a *part* of a book or other work.

Author and Title Analytic—The author and title of a separate work which is part of a larger work, such as an anthology.

AUTHOR ENTRY—The name of the author of a book or other work used as the filing name in the catalog; usually the main entry.

AUTHOR NUMBER—Part of a call number—letters and numbers assigned to a book to identify the author; also called a Cutter number.

AUTHORITY FILE—A record of names or terms used as catalog entries; maintained in order to keep the forms uniform.

BIBLIOGRAPHIC NOTE—A note on a catalog card indicating the presence of a bibliography in the work cataloged.

BIBLIOGRAPHY—A list of books, periodical articles, or other works.

BIOGRAPHEE—The subject of a biography; the person the work is about.

BIOGRAPHER—The author of a work about another person or persons.

BIOGRAPHY—A book or work about the life of a person or persons.

BOOK CARD—A card used to charge out a book or other work, identifying the work in circulation records.

BOOK NUMBER—Part of a call number, representing the title of a work.

BOOK POCKET—A small, heavy envelope pasted in a book to hold a card.

CALL NUMBER—The number (composed of letters, numbers, and symbols) used to identify and locate a book or other library item.

CASSETTE—A small box to contain film or magnetic tape.

CATALOG—A list of books and other materials arranged according to some definite plan; a list which represents the resources of a collection, a library, or a group of libraries.

CATCH or CATCHWORD TITLE—The distinctive part of the title of a book or other work—not the complete title.

CHARGING—The process of recording the loan of a book or other library item borrowed for use.

CLASS—A subject group or grouping; a subject number assigned an item.

CLASSIFICATION—The grouping of materials by subject or form, usually according to a scheme utilizing numbers and/or letters.

CLASSIFICATION SCHEDULE—The printed scheme of a particular system of classification.

CLOSE CLASSIFICATION—Classifying material in minute subdivisions of the subject.

CLOSED ENTRY—Catalog card or other listing giving complete bibliographical information; specifically applied to completed continuations, serials which have ceased publication, etc. (See *Open Entry*.)

CLOSED SHELVES or STACKS—Library area, not open to the public, where books are shelved.

CLOTHBOUND—Bound in cloth pasted over stiff boards.

COLLATION—Physical description of a work, giving such information as paging, number of volumes, illustrations, size, etc.

COLLECTION—A group of books or other materials; may refer to library's entire holdings or only to a special group or part.

COLLECTIVE TITLE—The inclusive title under which a group of books or other library materials is published, each of which may also have its own individual title.

COMPILER—One who assembles a collective work, such as a book comprising articles by various individuals.

CONTENTS NOTE—A listing of separate works or pieces included within a collective work.

CONTINUATION—A work issued as a supplement to one previously issued; a part issued in continuance of a book, a serial, or a series.

CONVENTIONAL TITLE—See *Uniform Title*.

COPY—One example of a book or other piece of library material; one object.

COPYRIGHT—The exclusive right granted by a government to publish a work during a specified period of years; a protection against others' copying it.

COPYRIGHT DATE—The date the copyright is granted.

CORPORATE BODY—A group or body of people acting as a unit, e.g., an association, institution, government unit.

CORPORATE ENTRY—The name of a corporate body used as a catalog entry.

CROSS REFERENCE—A referral from words or names not used to the forms used in a catalog, bibliography, or index.

CUTTER NUMBER—Letter plus the number taken from the Cutter or Cutter-Sanborn tables, assigned to an author's name to form part of the call number.

DATE—Any historical date. In cataloging, the publication or copyright date of a work or the birth and death dates of a person.

DATE DUE (SLIP)—Paper form pasted in a library book on which is stamped the date of the expiration of the loan period.

DESCRIPTIVE CATALOGING—Establishing the entries and providing the descriptive information given in the catalog.

DICTIONARY CATALOG—A catalog in which all the entries—authors, titles, and subjects—and their related references are arranged together in one general alphabet.

DISCARD—A book or other work officially withdrawn from a library, destroyed, or otherwise disposed of.

DUMMY CARD—A card, giving brief information, left in place of an official record removed from a file.

DUPLICATE—A book or other item identical with another in content, format, etc.; in library work, often used to indicate a copy of a work other than the first.

DUST JACKET—The paper covering (usually decorated) laid around a book.

EASY BOOK—A book, mostly composed of pictures, for young children.

EDITION—A distinctive text of a published work; each new edition implies additions to, or other changes in, the text.

END PAPER—The paper which lines the inside front and back covers of a book and also forms the flyleaves.

ENTRY—The word, name, or phrase under which a card is filed in the catalog; there are main entries, author entries, title entries, subject entries, series entries, etc.

FLYLEAF—The first or last sheet in a bound book, usually blank.

FORM HEADING—A made-up or formalized phrase used as entry for certain classes of materials, such as laws.

FORM TITLE—See *Uniform Title*.

FORMAT—The physical make-up of a work; size, binding, printing, etc.

GUIDE CARD—A card slightly higher than the catalog cards, carrying letters or names or words indicating the material directly behind it in the card catalog.

HANGING INDENTION—The form of a catalog card used when the title is the main entry and is the only line on the card coming to the first indention.

HEADING—Any word, name, or phrase placed at the head of a catalog card to indicate some special aspect of the book or other material.

HISTORY CARD—A catalog card which gives the history of successive names used by a person or an organization.

HOLDINGS—The library's collections.

IMPRINT—Publication information about a work: place, date, and publisher; usually found at the foot of the title page.

INDENTION—Distance from the left-hand side of the catalog card at which typing or printing begins.

INFORMATION FILE—A card file of references to sources of information on various topics. See also *Vertical File*.

INTERNATIONAL STANDARD BOOK NUMBER (ISBN)—A code number assigned by a publisher to a specific title or edition of a title. Used in ordering as an identification device.

INVENTORY—Taking stock of the library's collections.

JOINT AUTHOR, JOINT EDITOR—A person partially responsible for the content of a publication; usually not the first named on the title page.

LC—The Library of Congress.

LC CARD—A card prepared for the Library of Congress use; printed and sold to other libraries.

LEAF—A sheet containing two pages, one on each side, either or both of which may be blank, or may contain printing, writing, or illustrations.

LIBRARY BINDING—A special durable book or magazine binding to meet specifications and requirements of heavy library use.

LIBRARY SYSTEM—Two or more libraries affiliated for service; one may be administratively subordinate to the other, as a branch.

LIST PRICE—The price of a book or other publication listed by the publisher in catalogs and bibliographies, i.e., the retail price established by the publisher.

LOCATION SYMBOL (or MARK)—A letter, sign, or other symbol used on books or other materials in special collections which are shelved out of classification order.

MAIN ENTRY—A complete catalog record, usually the author entry, including all information necessary to identify the work. Usually contains the tracing of all other entries made for the work.

MATERIAL or LIBRARY MATERIAL—Inclusive term for books, periodicals, pamphlets, maps, films, etc.—all items which are legitimate acquisitions for a library's collections.

MICROFORM—A reproduction produced photographically or by other means in a size too small to be read by the unaided eye.

MONOGRAPHIC SERIES—Separate nonfiction works issued, possibly at different times, under a collective title; may or may not be a numbered series.

NOTE—A phrase or sentence added to the catalog card to explain a feature of the work cataloged.

OPEN ENTRY—A catalog entry for a serial, series, set, etc., which has not yet completed publication; certain information on the card is left incomplete.

OPEN SHELVES or STACKS—Shelves of books in an area open to the public.

OUT-OF-PRINT ITEM—All copies printed have been sold; item is no longer available from publisher.

OVERSIZE BOOK—A book too tall to shelve in its proper order.

PAGE—(1) In a book or other publication, one side of a leaf or sheet; (2) an assistant in a public library who does book shelving and other routine work.

PAMPHLET (BOX)—A pamphlet is a publication of less than 50 (or 100) pages, usually devoted to a specific subject; a pamphlet box is a container made of cardboard in which pamphlets are filed.

PAMPHLET FILE—See *Vertical File*.

PAPERBACK—A book bound in paper without the rigid boards used in cloth binding. Usually small in size.

PAPERBOUND BOOK—See *Paperback*.

PERIODICAL—"A publication with a distinctive title intended to appear in successive (usually unbound) numbers or parts at stated or regular intervals and, as a rule, for an indefinite time."—See *A.L.A. Glossary of Library Terms*.

PERIODICAL INDEX—An index to the contents of a periodical or group of periodicals.

PHONODISC—A recording of sound on a disc.

PHONOGRAPH RECORD—See *Phonodisc, Phonotape*.

PHONOTAPE—A recording of sound on tape.

PICTURE BOOK, JUVENILE—See *Easy Book*.

PLASTIC JACKET—A transparent book jacket made of Mylar or acetate to be applied to a book over the decorated book jacket.

POCKET BOOK—See *Paperback*.

PREBIND—To bind a book in special, durable "library binding" prior to library acquisition.

PREPARATIONS—That part of library work concerned with the physical preparation of a publication for library usage; includes such tasks as marking spine, pasting in pockets, stamping ownership, applying plastic jackets.

PROCESS SLIP—A slip of paper or card used by the cataloger in preparing information to be used in making catalog cards.

PROCESSING—Inclusive term for the work of acquiring, cataloging, preparing, and caring for library materials.

PSEUDONYM—Fictitious name used by an author.

PUBLICATION DATE—The year a work is published.

PUBLISHER'S CATALOG—A listing by a publisher of his current publications, publications in print, etc.

PUBLISHER'S SERIES—A series of separate works issued under a collective title, usually with some quality in common. Example: Landmark Books.

READING SHELVES—See *Shelf Reading*.

REBIND—To have a book rebound for library usage; the book which has been rebound.

RECORDING—See *Phonodisc, Phonotape*.

REFERENCE BOOK—(1) A book, such as encyclopedia or dictionary, used to obtain specific information quickly; (2) a book restricted to use within the library.

REGIONAL CENTER or LIBRARY—Office or library which supplies work, materials, or advice to affiliated or associated libraries.

REGIONAL PROCESSING—Processing work done centrally for two or more libraries.

REPLACEMENT—A copy of a publication to take the place of one lost or discarded.

REPRINT—(1) To print a published work again usually from the original type or plates; (2) a publication which is the same as an earlier one in content; the format may be the same or different. The term is sometimes used to mean a cheaper edition of an earlier work.

REVISE—(1) To check or review work done, e.g., to read copy, check filing, etc.; (2) to correct.

REVISED EDITION, REVISION—A publication containing new or changed material.

"SEE ALSO" REFERENCE—A referral from a name or term which has been used to others which are related to it.

"SEE" REFERENCE—A referral from a name or term not used to one which is to be found in a catalog or bibliography or index.

SEPARATE—A work cataloged and classified as an individual item, although published as part of another work or as one number of a monographic series.

SEQUEL—A work, complete in itself, but following in form or content after another; in fiction, a work continuing with the same characters, locale, etc.

SEQUENTIAL—A numbering following numerical order: 1, 2, 3, etc.

SERIAL—A publication issued in successive parts (which may or may not be numbered) and intended to be continued indefinitely; includes such items as periodicals, newspapers, reports, bulletins.

SERIES; SERIES ENTRY; SERIES NOTE—Separate, independent works issued, usually at different times, under a collective title; a catalog entry under the name of the series; a note on the catalog card identifying the individual work with the series.

SERIES TITLE—Name of the series to which a work belongs.

SET—A work of two or more volumes.

SHELF LIST; SHELF-LISTING—A file of cards, each representing a different title, arranged in the same order as are the books on the shelves; adding holdings of a library to the shelf-list card.

SHELF READING—Checking books on the shelves to ensure their proper arrangement.

SIZE—The height of a book; also the width if the book is of an unusual shape.

SPINE—The back of a book connecting the two covers, on which is usually lettered the title of the work.

STACKS—Standing shelves for books, usually of metal; the shelved collection; area in which materials are stored.

SUBJECT—A name, word, or phrase used as a catalog entry which indicates the subject content of the work cataloged.

SUBJECT ANALYTIC—A heading or catalog entry identifying the subject of a part of a work.

SUBJECT ENTRY—The catalog entry under a subject appearing at the top of the catalog card.

TITLE—The name of a work; in cataloging, the statement on the title page identifying the individual publication. "Full" title includes title, author, and additional information identifying the publication.

TITLE ANALYTIC—A catalog entry under the title of a part of a publication.

TITLE AND AUTHOR ANALYTIC—A catalog entry giving the title and then the author of a part of a publication.

TITLE ENTRY—The catalog entry under the title of a publication.

TITLE PAGE—The page, usually at the beginning of a book, identifying the individual work; gives the author, title, publisher, date, etc.

TITLE-PAGE NAME—Author's name in the form in which it appears on the title page.

TITLE REFERENCE—A catalog card referring from a form of a title not used as an entry to the one selected; the latter is usually a uniform title.

TRACINGS—Items listed on the main entry catalog card indicating other catalog entries made for the same work, i.e., the added entries and subject entries.

TRADE BIBLIOGRAPHY—A listing of the publications of one or more publishers.

UNION CATALOG—A catalog indexing the holdings of a library system, e.g., of a library and all of its branches and affiliates; or, of groups of various libraries.

UNIT CARD—One of a set of catalog cards, all of which are alike until the added entries are typed as headings.

VERTICAL FILE—A file of large drawers in which are arranged folders containing pamphlets, pictures, clippings, maps, etc.

VISIBLE FILE—A series of metal frames in which cards may be mounted with the headings visible one above another; used by libraries as a checking file for material received, and as the catalog record for periodicals.

VISIBLE INDEX—See *Visible File*.

VOLUME—The physical work complete in itself, whether a monograph which is part of a set or serial or an independent work.

WILSON CARDS—Catalog cards prepared, printed, and sold by The H. W. Wilson Company.

WITHDRAWAL—A work removed from the library's collections.

YEARBOOK—A work issued annually, e.g., an almanac.

For fuller definitions and other terms see the *A.L.A. Glossary of Library Terms* and *Anglo-American Cataloging Rules*.

Bibliography

Rules and Cataloging Tools

American Library Association. *A.L.A. Glossary of Library Terms; with a Selection of Terms in Related Fields.* Chicago, American Library Association, 1943. 159p.

Definitions of terms, including those for publishing and book making. Not always the same definitions as those used in Appendix III.

———*A.L.A. Rules for Filing Catalog Cards.* Pauline A. Seely, editor. 2d ed. Chicago, American Library Association, 1968. 260p.

Correlated with the new cataloging rules, these filing rules recommend as the basic order the straight alphabetical arrangement, with the exception of filing personal surname entries before other entries beginning with the same word. The rules are basically for a dictionary catalog, and primarily for manual filing.

———*A.L.A. Rules for Filing Catalog Cards.* Pauline A. Seely, editor. 2d. ed., abridged. Chicago, American Library Association, 1968. 94p.

Contains the same basic rules as the detailed code, cited above, but with much of the specialized and explanatory material omitted. This should be adequate for the small library.

Anglo-American Cataloging Rules. Prepared by the American Library Association, the Library of Congress, the Library Association, and the Canadian Library Association. North American Text. Chicago, American Library Association, 1967. 400p.

A revised cataloging code containing rules for entry and description. The rules are very detailed and many are inappropriate for a small library.

Association for Educational Communications and Technology. *Standards for Cataloging Nonprint Materials*. Rev. ed. Washington, National Education Association Publication Sales Section, 1971. 56p.

> Contains rules for cataloging nonprint materials, including some types of media not covered in other cataloging rules.

Baer, Eleanora A. *Titles in Series: A Handbook for Librarians and Students*. 2d ed. New York, Scarecrow Press, 1964. 2v.

> Includes approximately 40,000 book titles published prior to January 1963.

———— *Titles in Series: A Handbook for Librarians and Students*. 1st-2d Supplements to the 2d ed. Metuchen, N.J., Scarecrow Press, 1967-1971. 2v.

> Approximately 17,000 book titles included in the two supplements.

Code for Cataloging Music and Phono-Records. Prepared by a Joint Committee of the Music Library Association and the A.L.A. Division of Cataloging and Classification. Chicago, American Library Association, 1958. 88p.

> Includes chapters on simplified rules and phonodiscs.

Cutter, Charles A. *Alfabetic Order Table Altered and Fitted with Three Figures by Kate E. Sanborn*. (Obtained from the H. R. Huntting Company, Chicopee Falls, Massachusetts.)

> The table used by libraries with full call numbers, including author numbers. Not recommended for small libraries. A table is available also with two figures, but a library large enough to use Cutter numbers is most likely large enough to want the three-figure table.

Dewey, Melvil. *Decimal Classification and Relative Index*. 18th ed. Lake Placid Club, N.Y., Forest Press, Inc. of Lake Placid Club Education Foundation, 1971. 3v.

> Full classification scheme. Tables are divided and subdivided, supplying numbers for most specific subjects. Not necessary for small libraries.

———— *Abridged Dewey Decimal Classification and Relative Index*. Ed. 10. Lake Placid Club, N.Y., Forest Press, Inc. of Lake Placid Club Education Foundation, 1971. 529p.

> Abridged edition prepared specifically for schools and small public libraries. Recommended.

Kapsner, Oliver L., O.S.B. *Catholic Subject Headings*. 5th ed. Collegeville, Minn., St. John's Abbey Press. 1963. 488p.

> Used by libraries in Catholic schools and by parish libraries.

Library of Congress. *Classification. Class A-Z.* Washington, Govt. Printing Office, 1904 to date.

Classification schemes used by the Library of Congress. Not used except by large research libraries and highly specialized libraries.

———— *Decimal Classification Additions, Notes, and Decisions.* Washington, The Library, 1971 to date.

Known as "DC &," this publication, appearing at irregular intervals, gives information to supplement the DC classification between editions.

———— *Subject Headings Used in the Dictionary Catalogs of the Library of Congress.* 7th ed. Washington, Subject Cataloging Division, Processing Department, Library of Congress, 1966. 1432p. Supplements, 1964 to date.

LC subject headings appear on LC catalog cards. Although small libraries will not follow the list in detail, those using the cards may need the list to verify usage.

Lynn, Jeanette Murphy. *An Alternative Classification for Catholic Books.* 2d ed. rev. by Gilbert C. Peterson, S.J., with Supplement by Thomas G. Pater. Washington, Catholic University of America Press, 1965. 514p.

For use with DDC and LC classification; employed, if desired or required, by Catholic schools and parish libraries.

Rue, Eloise, and LaPlante, Effie. *Subject Headings for Children's Materials.* Chicago, American Library Association, 1952. 149p.

This was designed primarily for use in school libraries. It is out of date, and there are no provisions for its revision.

Sears, Minnie E. *Sears List of Subject Headings.* 10th ed., edited by Barbara M. Westby. New York, H. W. Wilson, 1972. 590p.

This list is the one used by schools and small public libraries—in fact, most public libraries. The headings are also those used in tools and bibliographies prepared for these libraries. Sears headings are used on Wilson cards. The list is fully revised about every five years. Recommended.

Smith, Elva S. *Subject Headings for Children's Books . . . .* Chicago, American Library Association, 1933. 235p.

Out of print and out of date, but parts still usable if combined with Sears.

Swain, Olive, comp. *Notes Used on Catalog Cards.* 2d ed. Chicago, American Library Association, 1963. 82p.

A classified collection of examples of notes used on catalog cards. Helps in phrasing notes and identifying information appropriately carried in them.

U.S. Government Printing Office. *Style Manual.* Rev. ed. Washington, Govt. Printing Office, 1967. 512p.

Every library needs a style book in its collection (either this one or the style manual published by the University of Chicago Press) for rules of punctuation, capitalization, spelling, and abbreviations, and usage in various languages.

Weihs, Jean Riddle. *Nonbook Materials: The Organization of Integrated Collections.* 1st ed. by Jean Riddle Weihs, Shirley Lewis, Janet Macdonald, in consultation with the CLA/ALA/AECT/EMAC/CAML Advisory Committee on the Cataloging of Nonbook Materials. Ottawa, Canadian Library Association, 1973. 107p.

Contains rules for cataloging nonbook materials developed according to the principles of the *Anglo-American Cataloging Rules.*

Bibliographies and Lists of Books Which Include Cataloging Information

American Book Publishing Record (BPR). New York, R. R. Bowker Company, 1960 to date.

A monthly periodical. Each issue contains the month's listings of books in *Publishers Weekly,* arranged according to Dewey classification. For each title the LC cataloging information is given: author, title, publisher, dates, subjects, etc. Has annual index volumes.

Book Review Digest. New York, H. W. Wilson Company, 1905 to date.

Bibliographic listing includes Dewey classification, subject headings, LC card number, and ISBN. Carries excerpts of reviews which are often helpful in determining subject and content of a book. The fiction grouping by subject in the annual and five-year indexes is particularly helpful in assigning subject headings to works of fiction.

The Booklist. Chicago, American Library Association, 1905 to date.

Semimonthly listings of publications appropriate for the small or medium-sized public library. Gives brief annotations and Sears subject headings, Dewey classification numbers, LC card numbers, and notation as to availability of Wilson cards.

Children's Catalog. 12th ed. New York, H. W. Wilson Company, 1971. 1156p.

List of selected titles appropriate for elementary schools and children's collections in public libraries. Includes Dewey classification, Sears subjects, grade level. New edition every five years; kept up to date with annual supplements.

Fiction Catalog. 8th ed. New York, H. W. Wilson Company, 1971. 653p.

Lists works of adult fiction found useful in libraries. Contains annotated author list and subject and title index. New edition every five years; kept up to date with annual supplements.

Junior High School Library Catalog. 2d ed. New York, H. W. Wilson Company, 1970. 808p.

Selected titles. Includes Dewey classification and Sears subject headings. New edition every five years; kept up to date with annual supplements.

Public Library Catalog. 5th ed., 1968. New York, H. W. Wilson Company, 1969. 1646p.

Selected titles, annotated and arranged according to Dewey classification; includes classification number, Sears subject headings, ISBN, and LC card number. New edition every five years; kept up to date with annual supplements.

Publishers Weekly. New York, R. R. Bowker Company, 1872 to date.

Each issue carries a list of books published that week in the United States. For each, LC cataloging is given. Cumulated monthly by subject in *American Book Publishing Record*.

Senior High School Library Catalog. 10th ed. New York, H. W. Wilson Company, 1972. 1214p.

Selected titles. Includes Dewey classification and Sears subject headings. New edition every five years; kept up to date with annual supplements.

———*Catholic Supplement*.

Includes additional books especially selected for Catholic schools. Not available separate from the *Senior High School Library Catalog*.

Manuals, Texts, and Guides

American Library Association. *Interim Standards for Small Public Libraries.* Chicago, The Association, 1962. 16p.
Standards adopted for libraries serving populations of less than 50,000.

———— *Minimum Standards for Public Library Systems, 1966.* Chicago, The Association, 1967. 69p.
This is essential for any public library.

———— *Standards for School Media Programs.* Chicago, The Association, 1969. 84p.
Includes media programming, selection, and organization of materials.

Barden, Bertha R. *Book Numbers: A Manual for Students, with a Basic Code of Rules.* Chicago, American Library Association, 1937. 32p.
Although old, this is the simplest and clearest explanation of the use of author numbers. It also includes a brief and simple system of numbering useful for the library or the collection needing numbers simpler than those in the Cutter tables.

Chicago Public Schools. *Cataloging and Processing Procedures for Elementary School Libraries: A Manual of Practice for the Chicago Public Schools.* Chicago, Chicago Teachers College, 1959. 130p.
This is an example of a manual designed for city or state systems. Others include those for New York City, North Carolina, and Georgia.

Dennis, D. D. *Simplifying Work in Small Public Libraries.* Philadelphia, Drexel Institute of Technology, 1965. 80p.
A practical manual to aid in planning and organizing the work.

Drazniowsky, Roman. *Cataloging and Filing Rules for Maps and Atlases.* Revised and expanded ed. New York, American Geographical Society, 1969. 92p.
Helpful for a library with extensive map collections.

Haykin, David J. *Subject Headings: A Practical Guide.* Washington, Govt. Printing Office, 1951. 140p.
A discussion of subject heading practice, particularly as applied to the Library of Congress headings. Needed only by the larger libraries using those headings.

Jackson, Ellen. *A Manual for the Administration of the Federal Documents Collection in Libraries.* Chicago, American Library Association, 1955. 128p.

Includes discussion of organization and system of classification and records. For the depository library or library with sizable documents collection.

Mary Annette, Sister. *Manual for Cataloging School Libraries.* 4th rev. ed. The Author, Briar Cliff College, Sioux City, Iowa, 1961. 97p.

A guide for libraries in Catholic schools or parishes.

Merrill, W. S. *Code for Classifiers; Principles Governing the Consistent Placing of Books in a System of Classification.* 2d ed. Chicago, American Library Association, 1939. 177p.

Some people find this, old as it is, helpful in learning how to classify a book.

Osborn, Andrew D. *Serial Publications: Their Place and Treatment in Libraries.* 2d ed., rev. Chicago, American Library Association, 1973. 434p.

Most comprehensive and up-to-date work on serials. Important to any library which has much material in serial form.

Pearson, Mary D. *Recordings in the Public Library.* Chicago, American Library Association, 1963. 153p.

A comprehensive work which includes much material about recordings, including classification, cataloging, and selection. Although written for the public library, it is valuable for any library collecting recordings.

Straugham, Alice. *How to Organize Your Church Library.* Westwood, N.J., Fleming H. Revell Company, 1962. 64p.

This booklet gives simple and practical methods for setting up and organizing a church library. Various denominations have also prepared manuals designed to help the church or parish library become of real service to the church, not just another—and inadequate—general library.

Strauss, Lucille J. *Scientific and Technical Libraries: Their Organization and Administration,* by Lucille J. Strauss, Irene M. Shreve, Alberta L. Brown. 2d ed. New York, Becker and Hayes, 1972. 450p.

A practical manual for special libraries.

H. W. Wilson Company. Directions and checklists for ordering Wilson printed cards.

A kit of material necessary for any library using Wilson cards.

Checklist of Individual Library Practices

The following checklist of decisions and practices, arranged in the same order as the chapters of this book, is designed to serve as a manual for the individual library. It is suggested that the cataloger, after reading through the entire book, study each chapter carefully, compare the practices recommended in it with those of his own library, then, deciding what is best or necessary for his library, check the items or note the information in the spaces indicated. By so doing, he will compile a record of the practices followed in his library. In the long run, this should save time and also make for greater consistency. Wherever pertinent, the author has indicated recommended practices with an asterisk. In some cases, however, the local situation may require different decisions; different practices may be preferred for different types of libraries; and some decisions are necessarily based on the individual library's responsibilities for service.

Chapter 1. Procedures and Preliminaries

BACKGROUND INFORMATION

1. Type of library (public, school, church, etc.) _____

2. Present size of community served (town, school, church)

   _____

3. Potential size of community _____

4. Other library resources in the community _____

   _____

5. Number of volumes now in the library _____

6. Potential size of the library (in volumes) _____

7. The library is part of a library system ____ yes ____ no

   the system _____

   the library's relationship to the system _____

   _____

   ____ a processing center is part of the system
   ____ the library belongs to the processing center

   nature of services received _____

   _____

8. The circulation system used in this library _____

   ____ book cards are used
   ____ date due slips are used

9. Lost book policy

_____ borrowers are charged

charges for lost books are _____

_____

10. Business records required to be kept by the library _____

_____

11. Readers served

_____ adults;   type of service _____

_____ children;   type of service _____

12. Shelving policy

_____ all books on open shelves

_____ some books in closed stacks; these include _____

_____

designation for books in closed stacks _____

13. Books are bought

_____ on contract

_____ by bids

_____ other means

14. Books are ordered

_____ daily   _____ semiannually

_____ weekly   _____ annually

_____ monthly   _____ irregularly

Explanation _____

_____

15. Gift books are accepted _____ yes _____ no

16. Different editions of nonfiction are kept _____ yes _____ no

17. Special collections which are specially housed _____

_____

     how cataloged and prepared _____

_____

_____

     how designated _____

Additional notes

Chapter 2. The Card Catalog

1. The library has a dictionary catalog

   *____ for adult use

   *____ for children's use

   ____ for both together

   ____ for other special groups, namely _____

   _____

2. Wilson cards, when available, are ordered

   *____ for adult books

   *____ for children's books

3. Library of Congress cards, when available, are ordered

   ____ for adult books

   ____ for children's books

   *____ when Wilson cards are not available

4. Cards are obtained from a processing center ____ or commercial service ____ or some other source, namely _____

   _____

   ____ for all books in the collection for which cards are
   available

   ____ when Wilson cards are not available

   ____ when LC cards are not available

5. For cards fully typed in the library, unit cards are used

   ____ always

   *____ only for main entry (of those in the catalog)

   *____ for shelf-list card

* Recommended practice

6. Tracings are indicated

　　*_____ on face of main entry card, if possible; on back if there is no room on face

　　_____ always on back of main entry card

　　*_____ on shelf-list card

7. Books cataloged and classified

　　_____ all books except _____

　　_____

　　_____ all hard-cover books

　　_____ paperbound books

　　*_____ decision is made on each work according to value and use

Additional practices

* Recommended practice

Chapter 3. The Main Entry

The individual library should record here any practices which, by policy, deviate from general usage.

Chapter 4. Added Entries

1. Title entries are made

    _____ for all titles

    _____ for all titles except those beginning with common words, namely _____

    _____

    _____ for all titles except those identical with subjects

    *_____ for catch titles

    _____ for inverted titles

2. Joint authors and joint editors

    If main entry is under the first of two authors or editors

    *_____ added entry is made for the second

    If main entry is under the first of three authors or editors

    _____ added entry is made only for the second

    *_____ added entries are made for the other two

    If main entry is under title of work by three or more authors or editors

    *_____ added entry is made only for the first author or editor

    _____ added entries are made only for the first two

    _____ added entries are made for all named on the title page

3. Entries for compiler, editor, illustrator, etc., are made

    *_____ only if their contribution is major

    _____ for all named on the title page

4. Entries are made for certain illustrators, namely _____

    _____

    _____

* Recommended practice

5. Title analytics are made

  *____ for all individual complete works

  ____ for works not covered by indexes

  ____ only for works listed on the title page

6. Author analytics are made

  *____ for all individual complete works

  ____ for works not covered by indexes

  ____ only for works listed on the title page

7. Subject analytics are made

  ____ for material of ____ pages or more

  *____ for separate works included in other works

  *____ for new or unusual material

8. Author and title analytics are made

  *____ for all individual complete works

  ____ for works not covered by indexes

  ____ only for works listed on the title page

9. Title and author analytics are made

  *____ for all individual complete works

  ____ for works not covered by indexes

  ____ only for works listed on the title page

10. Paging for analytics is given

  ____ for all analytics

  ____ only if the information is not shown elsewhere on the card

  ____ below the call number for all analytics

  ____ elsewhere on the card _____

* Recommended practice

11. Cards used for analytics

    *_____ unit cards if available

    *_____ short-form cards if cards are typed

12. Series cards are made

    _____ for all series

    _____ for all series except publishers' series

    _____ for some publishers' series, namely _____

    _____

    _____

    *_____ only for important series

*13. A file is kept of the names of those series for which series cards are made _____

Additional notes

Chapter 5. Form of Entry

1. For personal names

    _____ birth and death dates are used

    _____ dates are used in case of conflict of names

    _____ one form is adopted and always used

    _____ the title-page form is always used

    _____ the title-page form is used and is then followed for other entries (for the same person)

    _____ form is "established"; authorities used (in order) are _____

    _____

    _____

    _____ latest form of name is used; older entries are re-cataloged, if necessary

    *_____ "best-known" form is used if title pages vary

    *_____ pseudonyms are used as on the title page

    _____ best-known pseudonym is used for all works by an author

    _____ real name is always used if information is available

2. For corporate names

    _____ LC practice is followed

    *_____ Wilson practice is followed

    *_____ simple form is used

    _____ subdivisions are used

3. Conventional titles are used

    _____ generously

    *_____ sparingly

    _____ never

* Recommended practice

207

Additional notes

Chapter 6. Descriptive Cataloging

*1. The "by" phrase is used to supply needed information when the author statement on the title page differs from the name used in the main entry _____

2. Joint authors, etc., are included

   _____ only if important to the work

   _____ always

   _____ second author (if there are two) or second and third authors (if there are three or more named on the title page)

3. Place of publication is given

   _____ except for well-known publishers

   _____ except for fiction and easy books

   _____ only if other than New York

   *_____ never

4. Publisher is given

   *_____ except for fiction and easy books

   *_____ in short form

   _____ never

5. Date

   *_____ copyright date is preferred to imprint date

   _____ imprint date is preferred to copyright date

   _____ imprint date is used for all except fiction and easy books

6. Paging is used

   _____ always

   _____ never

   *_____ never for fiction or easy books

   *_____ for nonfiction

   *_____ only final Arabic number

* Recommended practice

209

7. Illustration notation is used

_____ never

*_____ restricted to "illus." and "map"

_____ restricted to _____

_____

8. Bibliography is indicated

_____ always

*_____ if sizable or important

_____ never

9. Series note is used

*_____ always

_____ never

_____ for selected series, namely _____

_____

_____

10. Contents notes are used

*_____ plentifully

_____ only for _____

_____

_____

11. Annotations are used

_____ always

*_____ only if available on printed cards

_____ never

12. Periodicals

*_____ are not cataloged

* Recommended practice

*_____ if cataloged, are cataloged under title at time of issue

_____ are cataloged under latest title

13. Other serials

    *_____ are cataloged under title at time of issue

    _____ are cataloged under latest title

14. Revised works

    *_____ for frequently revised works, open entries are plentifully used

    _____ frequently revised works are not cataloged

    *_____ certain revised works are not cataloged, namely

    _____

    _____

15. Size

    *_____ is not given

    _____ is given for certain types of material, namely

    _____

    _____

Additional notes

* Recommended practice

Chapter 7. Subject Cataloging

1. The subject headings list used is _____

*2. "See" references are made as indicated in headings list ____

*3. Additional "see" references are made as needed ____

*4. "See also" references are made as indicated in the headings list ____

5. Additional "see also" references are made ____

*6. Subject headings for prepared cards are checked against the library's catalog to see if subjects have been used ____

7. References are revised

    * ____ as each new subject is used

    ____ only as conflicts occur

    ____ periodically

8. General policy on subject work

* Recommended practice

Chapter 8. Classification of Books

(No practices are starred because different ones would be recommended for different types of libraries.)

1. The library classifies books according to _____

2. Dewey classification

   The class number is largely restricted to ____ digits

   Class numbers which are expanded include _____

   _____

   _____

   The Abridged Dewey is followed ____ yes ____ no

3. Reader interest group is used

   ____ for all circulating books

   ____ for certain categories, namely _____

   _____

   _____

   ____ for changing exhibits and is shown by _____

   _____

4. Adult fiction

   ____ is classified 813, 823, etc.

   ____ adult fiction is not classed

   ____ adult fiction in English is classed F

   ____ "Fiction" is used on catalog cards

5. Juvenile fiction

   ____ is classed 813, 823, etc.

   ____ is not classed

   ____ is classed jF

6. Picture books

    ____ are classed E

    ____ are classed ____

7. Individual biography is classed

    ____ 92

    ____ B

    ____ 920-929

    ____ other _____

8. Juvenile literature is indicated

    ____ by j

    ____ by other symbol(s) _____

9. Titles in both adult and juvenile collections are classed the same way   ____ yes   ____ no

    Exceptions _____

    _____

10. Author (Cutter) numbers are used

    ____ for all books

    ____ for all nonfiction

    ____ only for _____

    _____

11. Outsized books

    ____ are separately shelved

    ____ are indicated by _____

12. Materials separately shelved include _____

    _____

    _____

    They are designated by _____

13. Materials specially marked but not separately shelved include

_____

_____

14. A list of symbols is maintained _____ yes _____ no

It is kept _____

15. Other special practices

Chapter 9. Copy Identification

1. An accession book is maintained ＿＿ yes ＿＿ no

2. Accession record

    *＿＿ Every cataloged volume receives an accession number, but no accession record is maintained

    ＿＿ Every cataloged volume receives an accession number taken from an accession record

3. A copy number

    ＿＿ is assigned every copy (e.g., "copy 1")

    ＿＿ is assigned every copy except the first (e.g., "copy 2")

4. The accession number

    ＿＿ is numerical, 1 to infinity

    *＿＿ comprises date and number, e.g., ＿＿＿＿＿＿＿＿

    ＿＿ is some other combination, e.g., ＿＿＿＿＿＿＿＿

5. The identification is ＿＿ written *＿＿ stamped ＿＿ typed

    *＿＿ on the book card

    *＿＿ on the pocket

    ＿＿ on the shelf list

    ＿＿ in the book page ＿＿

6. The identification is assigned

    *＿＿ as soon as the book is cleared by the order process

    ＿＿ while the book is being shelf-listed

    ＿＿ after the book is fully prepared

    ＿＿ other practice ＿＿＿＿＿＿＿＿＿＿＿＿＿

    ＿＿＿＿＿＿＿＿＿＿＿＿＿＿＿＿＿＿＿＿

* Recommended practice

Additional notes

Chapter 10. The Shelf List

1. Type of card used for shelf list

   *____ unit card

   ____ shortened form, with the following information included _____

   _____

2. Price

   (Recommended practices are for public libraries only; price is not used in school libraries.)

   *____ price is given on shelf-list card

   ____ real (discount) price is used on shelf-list card

   *____ list price is used on shelf-list card

   ____ price recorded is list price raised to next even dollar

   ____ price is coded, as follows: _____

   _____

3. Variant editions

   *____ variant editions are shown in accession information for fiction and easy books

   ____ illustrator variation for fiction and easy books is shown on shelf-list card for all illustrators

   *____ illustrator variation is shown for selected illustrators, namely _____

   _____

4. Date and source of acquisition are shown on shelf-list cards

   ____ yes   *____ no

* Recommended practice

218

Additional notes

Chapter 11. Catalog Cards and Catalog Maintenance

Notes on library's practices

Chapter 12. Cataloging Services

Notes on library's practices

Chapter 13. *Physical Preparation of Material*

(No specific practices are recommended since libraries must meet circulation and service requirements.)

1. Price

     Information is put in book ____ yes ____ no

     Price is lettered in book on page ____

     Price used

         ____ list

         ____ real

         ____ coded; code is determined by _____

         _____

         ____ (coded) price is included on book card

         ____ (coded) price is included on book pocket

2. Call number

     ____ penciled on page ____

     ____ lettered on spine, ____ inches from bottom

     ____ vertically lettered on spine, top to bottom

     ____ vertically lettered on spine, bottom to top

3. Lettering device used _____

4. Discs are applied to spine to indicate _____

    _____

5. Lettering is shellacked ____ yes ____ no

6. Book is stamped with name of library on _____

7. Book pocket is pasted _____

8. Date due slip is pasted _____

9. Jackets are applied with _____

10. Plastic jackets are used on _____

    _____

11. Supplements, etc., are removed from book _____ yes _____ no

    _____ filed in vertical file

    _____ filed elsewhere: _____

    _____

    _____ disposition of supplement is noted on pocket

12. Other preparations

Chapter 14. Audio-visual and Other Nonbook Materials

Material	Where housed	How arranged	Classification symbol used	If cataloged, under what entry
Motion pictures				
Filmstrips				
Slides				
Microforms				
Phonodiscs, -tapes, Musical				
Phonodiscs, -tapes, Nonmusical				
Pamphlets				
Clippings, etc.				
Pictures				
Models, Dioramas, Realia				
Games and Kits				
Maps				
Manuscripts, Letters, etc.				
Music				
Periodicals/Serials				
Newspapers				
Paperbacks				
Other physical objects				

a gen- sep- talog	Cards bordered or stamped	Cards in general shelf list or special file	Grade or age indicated	Physical preparation	Statistics kept

Chapter 15. Keeping Records Up to Date

1. Records for names

     _____ authority record is maintained for all names used

     _____ authority record is maintained only for names which require cross references

     _____ cross references are indicated as tracings on main entry cards

2. Records for subjects

     *_____ printed list of subjects is checked for headings used

     _____ authority card record is maintained for subjects used

3. Names and subjects are combined in one authority file _____

4. Classification decisions

     *_____ are written in the printed scheme

     _____ are recorded on cards

     _____ are recorded in a notebook

5. Serial cataloging decisions

     _____ are recorded on separate cards

     _____ are recorded on shelf-list cards

     *_____ are recorded in serials check file

6. Illustrator entry decisions

     _____ are recorded on separate cards

     *_____ are recorded in a list

     _____ are recorded in name authority file

7. Other authority files maintained _____

   _____

   _____

* Recommended practice

8. Order cards used in cataloging work

    *_____ call number for added copies or volumes is given on order card

    *_____ order card is left in book for cataloging use

9. Dummy cards

    _____ dummy is left in shelf list for cards withdrawn for use

    _____ order card is used as dummy

10. Open-entry cards

    _____ all cards for open entry are changed to show additions

    *_____ only main entries for open-entry cards are changed to show additions

11. Recataloging and reclassification policy

    *_____ kept to a minimum

    _____ never done

    _____ always done for any change

    *_____ subject changes for new terminology

    *_____ subject changes for new concepts or meanings

    *_____ reclassification to break up too much material within a class

    _____ reclassification to conform to new edition of the scheme

    *_____ reclassification to show new concepts or meanings

    *_____ reclassification to avoid conflict

    _____ recataloging to show all name changes

    *_____ recataloging only to avoid conflict

    _____ other policies on change _____

_____

* Recommended practice

12. Withdrawal of cards from catalog

*_____ cards for discarded books are withdrawn immediately

_____ cards for discarded books are withdrawn _____

_____

_____ cards for missing items are withdrawn immediately

*_____ cards for missing items are withdrawn after one year

_____ cards for missing items are withdrawn after six months

13. Records for books ordered for replacement are shown by

*_____ flagging the shelf-list card

_____ flagging the order card

_____ other practice _____

_____

14. Inventory is taken

_____ annually

_____ every three years

_____ every five years

_____ at other intervals _____

15. Statistics kept (see pages 128-130 and also checklist for Chapter 14, page 225)

_____

_____

_____

_____

* Recommended practice

Additional notes

Index